D1707150

THE CHILDREN'S NURSE

*A WWII Historical Survival
Novel Based on a True Story*

EHUD REGEV

Producer & International Distributor
eBookPro Publishing
www.ebook-pro.com

THE CHILDREN'S NURSE:

A WWII Historical Survival Novel
Based on a True Story

EHUD REGEV

Translation: Ziona Sasson
Editor: Dalia Talmon

Contact: ehud.regev@gmail.com

ISBN 9798858785712

*Dedicated with love
to my wife Yehudit*

CONTENTS

4. WARSAW 1947   175

5. ISRAEL   246

AUTHOR'S NOTE

The life story of my mother, Miriam (Merie) Gerber, blessed be her memory, is the source of inspiration and the basis for the events and characters portrayed in this book.

The book focuses on World War II and the years that followed, her escape from Poland, up to her immigration to *Eretz Yisrael*, the Land of Israel, in 1949.

This is a work of fiction, in which facts intertwine with imagination, and historical accuracy is ornamented with the author's poetic license. Many details mentioned in this book reflect the true reality of that time, as I came to know it, whereas other details are the figment of my imagination – each according to its relevance and purpose.

As to the main characters, although they describe actual people and their real names, they are mostly fictitious and do not necessarily describe a true reflection of their lives.

Research of the historical events mentioned in this book relied on numerous sources. However, since the book was written decades after my mother's death, there were many gaps which needed to be filled in. This helped me achieve my integrate poetic license into the historical facts, tapping into my imagination as best I could, to reinforce the described reality. And yet, even though this story touches on actual historic events, it does not constitute historical research.

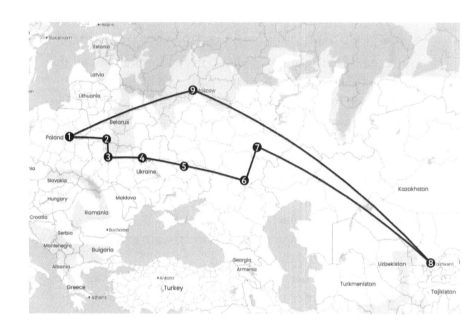

1	Warsaw	**4**	Kiev	**7**	Saratov
2	Pinsk	**5**	Kharkov	**8**	Tashkent
3	Rovno	**6**	Stalingrad	**9**	Moscow

PROLOGUE

It is the summer of 1958. I am twelve years old and have just graduated from the elementary school in Kibbutz Shaar Hagolan. We celebrated the end of the school year with our parents a few days ago.. I played my violin in a short violin and piano recital accompanied by the renowned composer Chaim Barkani, for which I was highly praised.

That was the last time I ever played the violin.

Ever since we made *aliyah*, immigrated to Israel in late 1949, my parents lived apart.

The day after the school celebration, my mother and I flew to Warsaw to meet my father. He was a history professor and deputy rector of Warsaw University.

After an exhausting thirty-six hour trip, while we were still in the taxi leaving the airport, my father told us his friend, the second secretary and cultural attaché of the Israeli Embassy, and his wife, will be waiting to meet us that same evening at home.

"He's a very good friend of mine and wants to meet you," my father said.

"What's his name?" My mother asked.

"Zvi," Father replied, "Zvi Netzer."

At eight o'clock that evening, the doorbell rang. Mother went to the door with me closely behind her, feeling curious. The door opened and a man and woman stood on the doorstep.

"Alexander!" Mother cried, stunned The man placed a finger over his mouth and nodding his head to indicate 'no,' said in an official tone, "Hello, Mrs. Gerber, I am Zvi Netzer from the Embassy, and this is my wife."

Mother immediately pulled herself together and said, "Rafal told me you would be coming this evening. Please come in."

"Rafal," she called out, her face revealing nothing of her inner turmoil, "Your guests from the embassy have arrived."

It was then, that I understood for the first time, that my mother's life story was made up of a myriad of small particles which held within it secrets, most of which most likely she had kept to herself.

1.

THE ESCAPE
FROM WARSAW - 1939

Chapter One:
Warsaw in flames

Merie stood at the window of the Surgery Department on the second floor of the Orthodox Jewish Hospital in Warsaw, the capital city of Poland, carrying a pile of sheets for the Emergency Room, which had been transferred to the basement floor. Her black hair was carefully tucked under a white cap lined with a black stripe along its edge, indicating she was a registered nurse. She had on a dazzling white uniform and apron, but as she gazed out the window at the ruins, she was worried. She thought about her classmates from the *Tarbut* Gymnasium in Pinsk. Most of them had joined a group that immigrated to *Eretz Yisrael*, the Land of Israel, and so were spared these war-ridden sights. They wrote her about the kibbutz they had set up in the Jordan Valley near the Sea of Galilee. She had always believed she would join them. After all, she spoke fluent Hebrew and fully believed that all Jews should build their homeland in *Eretz Yisrael*.

On the first day of the month, German forces had invaded Poland, inundating it, as they advanced toward Warsaw.

To the Poles' horror, two weeks later, the Russian army also invaded their land from the east, and within days had settled along the Bug River.

Since graduating from Nursing School six years earlier, Merie specialized in treating children and worked in the hospital's Pediatric Intake and Emergency Ward. The hospital consisted of eight, three to four-story buildings, and was located in a forest in the heart of the Czyste neighborhood.[1] Now the Pediatric Ward stood empty. The sick and wounded children were transferred down to the ground floor and the basement of building No.8, to shield them from the German bombings. During the past few days Warsaw remained the last Polish stronghold not yet conquered by the Germans, but the Germans were determined to crush the city. Machine guns incessantly fired on the buildings, and heavy bombers and Stuka diving planes swooped down on every nook and cranny.

Merie clutched the sheets as she looked on what seemed to her as the end of the world. Suddenly, a shrill sound interrupted her thoughts, the sirens of diving planes circling over the hospital. A bomb hit building No.7, and Merie was thrown down by the blast. She got up quickly and ran, practically flying down the stairs to the basement.

She knew that within minutes the emergency room would fill up with the wounded.

At the entrance to the emergency room, she saw Dr. Mirovsky. "Doctor!" she called. "We must get ready for another wave of injured!" Dr. Mirovsky looked at her tiredly. "As

---

1   The hospital still stands today in the same place in Warsaw. Its name was changed to Spitzal Wolski.

if we haven't had enough injured untill now," he said as they entered the Pediatric Surgical Emergency Ward. Children of all ages lay in rows of beds and on blankets spread out on the floor. Frightened parents stared at Merie. Chaos and confusion were everywhere. Merie quickly smoothed out her uniform, then went over to Stephan, a six-year-old boy who came in only a few hours earlier with an open fracture in his left leg. Like many other children, he too was brought to the hospital without his parents. She placed her hand on Stephan's head as he cried out in pain, stroked him gently and whispered, "Stephan, dear, I'm so sorry you're in pain... you'll be taken care of very soon, I'm going to find the doctor."

"Where is Mother?" Stephan asked as he looked at her with his big eyes. Merie had no answer. She had to find Dr. Mirovsky and continue to treat the other children. She was exhausted. Everyone was scared. The room was filled with the children's crying and shouts of pain. She too wanted to cry. Dr. Mirovsky was attending to a boy with a broken leg and shoulder. The boy was screaming with pain and Merie stroked his cheek. "Here, have some water," she handed him a glass. "Dr. Mirovsky, what shall we do about the boy over there," she pointed towards Stephan. "He has an open fracture and..."

"He has to be taken down to surgery, I can see it from here... but we're all out of anaesthetics, which wee sent for to the big civil hospital so hopefully we'll be able to renew surgery this evening. I'll finish up here and then we'll set his leg. Let's hope for the best." Dr. Mirovsky once again gave her that same tired look.

"And what about the sedatives?" she asked.

"We're short on that too, but maybe there are some morphine ampules still left."

Merie walked over to the narcotics cabinet where she found the last few ampules. "Stephen, dear, I'm going to give you a shot so you won't be in pain," she said as she held the morphine syringe in her hand. She stroked his hair and he gazed at her with his large, moist eyes and nodded. She then gently injected the sedative into the muscle, and stroked his head until he closed his eyes.

Once again, the ground beneath them shook with a heavy burst of shellfire that landed on the buildings near the hospital. While attending to the children, Merie thought about her girl-friends – Pola, Batya, Magda and Clara. If she hadn't been forced to stop her high-school studies and move to the nursing-school in Warsaw, she wouldn't have been exposed to all this human suffering. However, instead of joining her girlfriends and leaving with them, she had no choice at the time but to help support her parents and pay for her young brother Godel, nicknamed Gadi's studies. Gadi had graduated from high school in Pinsk a year earlier. During her last year of studies in Warsaw, she met Rafal, a history Ph.D. student and a Communist, who captured her heart. They got married and lived in a small apartment. Now he was making his way over to the Russian side while she stayed behind, praying for his safety.

Chapter Two:
The German Occupation

The battles ended in late October of 1939. The Polish army lay down its arms, the Polish government announced its surrender and the people of Warsaw anxiously awaited what was to come. A long motorcycle convoy rode down *Jerozolimskie*, the city's main avenue with an armed soldier on the sidecar of every motorcycle. A tank column followed the convoy, ending with an autocade of trucks filled with soldiers. The armed forces split up from the main avenue, and overtook the government buildings, radio stations, police HQ, military camps and hospitals, flying red flags with a white circle and a black swastika in its center on top of the buildings.

The German army marched through Warsaw's main streets in a triumph parade, escorting Hitler as he rode through the city in his open car. The occupation statutes were efficiently displayed in German and the *Generalgouvernement* was established – a General Governorate for the occupied Polish region, turning the Polish regions not annexed to Germany or Russia, into a German zone of occupation.

Merie ran frantically through the hospital corridors. The long siege, the bombings and destruction of the water and sewage systems promoted epidemics whose victims were funneled to the hospital wards. Like all the doctors and nurses, Merie too was forbidden to leave the hospital premises by order of the German forces. It has been a month since she had stepped outside the closed campus.

As she was hurrying to the children's ward, her fingers groped for the note in her apron pocket. Had she made the right decision to stay in Warsaw? As the war wore on, both she and Rafal understood that as a Jewish member of a Communist group cell, his chances of survival were poor. They were well aware that he could not pass as a Pole. "Your looks announce you're a Jew loud and clear!" she used to tease him, referring to his dark skin and black hair. Rafal asked her to join him, to cross the border together with him. "I can't leave the children in the middle of a war," Merie answered. "But you have no choice in the matter."

"Your devotion to the children won't help you with the Germans," he said. "Besides, Henrik is already in Brest and all my other comrades are planning to do the same."

"Yes, but I belong to the *Hashomer Hatzair* [the Socialist Zionist Youth Movement], and besides I..."

"You really think the Germans care what you do? Merie, for God's sake, they're killing Jews because they're Jews, and they're killing Communists because they're Communists." Merie remained silent. She knew this moment would come. "Tonight a truck that's smuggling out escapees leaves for Brest," Rafal said as he gazed into Merie's dark eyes. "Here's a note with Petka's phone number. Take it. If you decide to escape to the Russian side, call him and he'll add you to the group or connect you with another smuggler." They kissed briefly, a quick hug, and he disappeared into the night.

Merie had learned from the other nurses that there was a way to leave the hospital clandestinely, through the basement, which now served as a morgue. There was a long, narrow window close to the ceiling that could be opened, and through it, one could roll out onto the street. The nurses would secretly leave the hospital through that window to visit their children and always returned with horrific descriptions of the city's ruins.

A full month had passed since the ban on leaving the hospital went into effect. Merie missed her parents and her brother. She knew she wouldn't find Rafal in their apartment in the Old City, but she just had to see for herself that their building was still standing. She slipped out through the window onto the street that she knew so well. Now it was unrecognizable.

The facades of many buildings were shaved away, so she could look into the interiors, into the empty rooms that once housed people and vibrant lives. She stood before one building, gazing into what seemed like a children's room: Broken beds, toys and piles of children's clothing. Blood stains everywhere testified to the horrors. She continued towards their apartment.

A large group of ultra-Orthodox Jews in their traditional dress was removing the rubble under the watchful eye of German soldiers. She asked one of the Jews why they were doing this and his answer hit her like a bolt of lightning. "You don't know? The Germans have forbidden all Jews to do any business-related work, instead we're forced to clear the rubble from the city's ruins." Overwhelmed and with her legs nearly failing her, she rushed to the apartment. She was relieved to see that the building was still standing. She opened the main door and her tears fell uncontrollably. "Hurry," a voice in her head said. She quickly packed a knapsack with a change of clothes and some other items she needed at the hospital, locked the door and walked out. As she reached the main street, she saw a German officer and three soldiers huddled around a group of thick-bearded Jews. They grabbed the beard of one of them, pushed him down to the ground, then kicked him repeatedly, while one of them held his beard, and with one violent yank, wrenched it off the beard with some of the flesh. The old man's screams were heard throughout the street, while the Poles who stood around watching, snickered. The other Jews sought a place to hide lest they be next in turn. There was no one to help him. That was the new regime, soldiers who beat old men.

Merie's was horrified. She decided at once not to return to Czyste and looked for a public phone. Her hand fingered the note in her pocket.

She found a public phone booth at the street corner and with a shaking finger, dialed the number on the note.

"Petka?" she asked when the phone was picked up at the other end.

"Who is this?"

"My name's Merie," she said. "I got your number from Rafal, my husband, he crossed over with you a month ago."

Silence at the other end. "Where do you work?"

"At the Czyste Hospital," Merie answered in a shaky voice.

Again, silence. "Yes, I'm Petka, and Rafal talked about you. What do you want?"

"To join you on the Russian side."

"Now it's much more difficult and dangerous," Petka said.

"I know," Merie answered, "but I can't stay here."

"Can you leave tonight?" he asked.

"Yes."

"Okay. Prepare one knapsack and your papers. A vehicle will stop to pick you up at the corner of the main bridge over the Vistula River further down Jerozolimskie Avenue at exactly five p.m. If you're there, we'll pick you up. Understood?"

"Yes, understood."

"Oh, and the price is two hundred zloty."

"Rafal said the price is a hundred zloty."

"So he said… but things have changed. The risks are greater. Tomorrow, if it's at all possible to cross over to the Russian side, the price will go up to three hundred zloty."

"I'll be there," she said.

Merie went back to their apartment. The narrow streets and the center square swarmed with German soldiers celebrating loudly and drinking beer. Merie stumbled as she entered the building and quickly ran up the stairs. As soon as she shut the door behind her, she sat down on the couch to catch her breath as she regained her composure. Who could ever have imagined Warsaw like this, who could have known that the Jews' lives would be in such danger.

Their entire savings were hidden away in the clothes closet in the bedroom, it came to eight hundred and ninety zloty, two hundred would have to go to Petka. She took out two hundred zloty, which she rolled up, and hid in her bra, while the rest she shoved into her skirt pocket. She just had a few more things to gather into the knapsack that would contain her entire life. There were still a few hours left before her meeting with the smuggler. She lay down on her bed, perhaps for the last time, and decided to take a quick nap before the long journey ahead of her. Is she doing the right thing by leaving the hospital? As the thoughts ran through her mind, she stroked the soft sheets and thought of little Stephan, and of the children she was so attached to. An hour later, she stood up and finished packing the very last items into her knapsack. Glancing for the last time at Rafal's and her love nest she knew she couldn't stay there any longer. She locked the door and headed downstairs, just as Anna, who had studied with Rafal at Warsaw University, was coming up to her apartment.

"How are you, Merie?" she asked. "I haven't seen you around. Where are you going with that knapsack?"

"I came from Czyste to check out the apartment and take a change of clothing," Merie said. "I was shut up there for a month," and then suddenly she hugged Anna and said, "I'll see you after the war."

As Anna watched her as she quickly went down the stairs, Merie stepped out to the street. She turned around, looked at the house that was home to Rafal and her for the past few years, and then continued down the narrow streets of the old city. It was three o'clock in the afternoon when she passed by the Polish Royal Palace which was now covered with red flags with swastikas. She continued down Krakowskie Przedmieście Street past the luxurious Bristol Hotel, whose white structure was always prominent, but has been confiscated and covered with Nazi flags, turned into the Occupation's administration center. She kept walking down Nowy Świat Street, filled with restaurants and cafés which, like in the old city, were packed with jubilant German soldiers, as well as Polish residents. Merie quickened her step towards Jerozolimskie Avenue that led to the river and turned to the Poniatowskiego Bridge over the Vistula River.

At precisely five o'clock, a canvassed pickup truck would stop and she would disappear inside it.

Chapter Three:
The Escape From Warsaw

It was nearly five o'clock when Merie stood at the junction of Jerozolimskie Avenue and Poniatowskiego Bridge. The road was empty except for vehicles filled with German soldiers. People were afraid to wander around. Strong gusts of wind blew in from the river and the city was covered with heavy clouds. A shiver ran through Merie's body. She too would be leaving Warsaw in just a few minutes.

At precisely five o'clock, a canvas-covered pickup truck stopped next to her. A man of slight build wearing a heavy coat and a woolen cap jumped out of the driver's cabin. "Merie?" he asked.

"Petka?" she asked in return.

"There's no time for quiz games," Petka said. "Do you have the money?"

Merie put her hand under her coat and pulled out the bills. "Two hundred zloty, like you said," she replied. "You're not going to count it?" she asked as he shoved the roll of bills into his pocket.

"No, no time for that. We must reach Siedice before curfew." Petka raised the canvas flap. "Quick, put your foot here on the step." Merie did as he told her and leaped into the truck. It was pitch black, but the sound of breathing revealed that there were other people in there. Before she had a chance to sit down on the narrow bench, the truck hurtled forward unto the bridge across the river.

A strong wind swayed the truck from side to side during the ride over the bridge, but no one made a sound. Merie could smell the fear, the odor of sour sweat that pervaded the stuffy space. It began to rain which dripped down through the canvas roof.

"Hi, I'm Merie," she whispered to the person next to her.

"Shhh..." a voice shushed from the darkness, "wait till we cross the bridge and get away from the city."

The truck came to a sudden stop and took a sharp turn to the right. Outside, shouts in German were heard, "Halt!" The thunderous sounds of tanks and regiments moving along the road were clearly heard prevailing the silence of the stopped truck.

"Where to?" a voice said in German mixed with broken Polish.

"To Siedice," Petka answered.

"Wait here," the German said. "Another convoy will be leaving after this convoy. You'll be able to join it." The German moved away and Petka could be heard murmuring to himself in Polish, "Of course, officer, there has to be order."

After fifteen minutes that seemed like an eternity, the convoy began to move.

A man sitting opposite Merie peeked out through a hole in the canvas and said, "Unbelievable, but right behind us is a German military police motorcycle with a sidecar. Are you aware of that, Petka?"

Petka glanced through the side mirror and answered indifferently, "Yeah, that's how we'll get through the blockades at Siedice. After that, we'll see." Merie also found a slit in the canvas, which she poked with her finger and peeked out. The sky was cloudy and her eyes focused on the tall green trees that rushed by. The rain grew stronger and tapped on the canvas roof. She looked at Warsaw's houses as they rushed by and asked herself if she would ever see them again.

The German convoy was moving slowly. After an hour and a half, they reached the outskirts of Siedice. The motorcycle that brought up the rear now drove passed the truck and rushed to the front of the convoy. Petka took advantage of the moment and veered to the right unto a dirt road. The convoy continued eastward while the truck headed south. They traveled slowly for about half an hour in the rain until they reached a farm. Petka parked the truck in the barn and shut the motor.

"You can get out and stretch a bit," he said. "The first leg of our journey is behind us. We'll spend the night here and continue to Brest in the morning."

A small kerosene lamp lit the barn. Though its light was dim, it was the first time the truck's fellow travelers were able to look at each other. Besides Merie, there were three men and a woman, all in their twenties, all members of a Communist Party cell, students at Warsaw University, as Merie later learned. Zosia and Roman were history students and knew Rafal, and Marik and Radek were physics students.

The group settled down in a circle and shared their experiences of the German occupation in Warsaw, of ghastly encounters with German soldiers. Merie told them about the old Jewish man she saw in the street just the day before. "It was Rafal who made the initial contact with the smuggler Petka," Zosia said and sighed. "He joined the first run, then returned to tell us about the smuggling route that opened to the east, and gave us Petka's phone number," Roman added.

"On the second trip, Rafal crossed over to the Russian side," Merie said. "He asked me to join him, but I wasn't ready to leave the hospital."

"I hope you're not too late," Zosia said.

"And I just hope we make it in one piece," Radek added.

Petka suggested they all go to sleep. "We have a long day ahead of us," he said. "We'll head out early, before sunrise."

They lay down on the hay piles beside the truck, covered themselves with their coats and fell asleep immediately. Silence filled the barn.

At four a.m., Petka awoke the group. He drove the truck out of the barn, pulled it up close to one of the sheds and asked the men to load twenty sacks of potatoes from the shed unto the truck. He then gathered the group and said, "Here's my story, I deliver potatoes to the market at Terespol, on the western side of the river. That borderline was set between the Russians and the Germans. The problem is there are two blockades along the way. If we cross them and reach the river in one piece, I have connections with a boat owner who will take you across the river to the Russian side. The sacks of potatoes are my excuse for traveling on the roads, and you are a group of students who were trapped in the city. Since studies at Warsaw University were stopped, you're on your way home until the university reopens. Is this story clear to you?" Everyone nodded in agreement.

"When I say so," he glanced at the men, "place one sack of potatoes on the ground."

"What for?" Marik asked.

"Actually, the potatoes will serve as bribery at the blockades. The German army hasn't yet established itself logistically and for the German soldiers a sack of potatoes is a virtual party," Petka pulled his coat close.

The group got on the truck. The twenty sacks of potatoes took up half the space, so and the group had to huddle together. Petka climbed unto the driver's seat and they moved out. They moved slowly along the narrow paths between the farms, as the skies grew darker and the clouds gathered quickly. Despite the severe cold, the strong winds and the rain the group felt optimistic. As Petka said, "The colder and wetter it gets, the less determined the soldiers are to come out of their sheltered post and check the passengers."

The truck turned unto the main road that bypassed Siedice, the city where the night before they had pulled away from the German convoy. As Petka got on the main road heading towards Brest, he picked up speed. Half an hour later, the truck slowed down and then stopped. In the back of the truck, silence fell. A German soldier presented himself as the blockade commander and asked Petka to step out of the truck. He asked what the purpose of his trip was. Merie understood what they were saying. Petka explained about the potatoes and the students that he was returning home. Then the sergeant flashed his light and asked to check the inside of the truck.

"Please, Sergeant," Petka said and raised the flap of the canvas covering. The sergeant flashed his light on the passengers' faces and then directed his flashlight to the potato sacks. Petka instructed Marik, in Polish, to remove one sack from the truck. "This is for you, Sergeant," he said. The German nodded and Petka carried it to the blockade tent. Returning to the driver's seat, he let out a deep breath and started up the engine. The passengers' fear and anxiety dissipated somewhat with the truck's renewed motion. "I wonder how far we'll get," Radek said.

"If we ever get there…," Roman added.

"I'm so worried about my parents in Horodno," Merie said, "that's where I'm heading."

"It's a good place to be these days," Zosia replied. "Why are you worried?"

"Since the war started, we've had no contact as with my brother, they're not young anymore…"

Once again, the truck slowed down and a soldier asked Petka where he was heading. Petka repeated his cover story. This time, the German soldier shouted, "Everyone out!"

Petka climbed out of the driver's seat quickly, lifted the canvas cover and told everyone to get down. He was clearly worried. Merie stepped out of the truck last and looked at the German officer's hat with a silver skull insignia on it. He was an infamous SS.

"Who are you and what are you doing here?" he shouted. Petka tried once more to explain that he was on his way to the weekly market, but the officer shouted, "Get in line!" Merie stood next to Zosia. "Partisans are you?" he asked. Everyone nodded 'No.' The officer ordered his soldiers to unload the potato sacks and search for ammunition. After all the sacks were removed and no ammunition was found, the officer turned to the group. "I'm going to search each of you. If I find any weapon on any one of you, he will be executed immediately. Do any of you have a weapon?"

"No!" they all answered as one.

"Open your coat," the officer barked at Marik. Two soldiers aimed their guns at the group and the officer nodded his head slightly. One of the soldiers did a body search on Marik, then the officer nodded to the other soldier, who shoved his gun into Marik's back. Marik screamed in pain and fell on his face. The officer turned to Roman and then to Radek. Both of them were beaten and fell down on the muddy ground. Zosia was next. The soldier did a thorough body search on her, focusing on her breasts, thighs and between her legs. When he was done, the other soldier hit her in the stomach and she too dropped down on the ground, crying out in anguish. Merie was similarly searched, and the soldier then took the butt of his rifle and hit her hand and left shoulder. The pain seared her body but she remained standing.

"Everyone, on your feet!" the officer said in Polish. "Any Jews among you?" The group members quickly stood up and nodded in the negative. "Any Communists?" Again, everyone nodded in the negative. "Okay," he said, this time in German. "This is a closed military zone. You will leave the potato sacks here and each of you will return to where you came from. If I see any of you again, you will be executed. Is that clear?"

"Yes, Sir," Petka said, his head lowered. He knew he mustn't argue.

Chapter Four:
The German Side Of The Bug River

The truck meandered its way back towards Siedice, empty of the potatoes but carrying six young men and women, beaten, in pain and very worried about their future. Their clothes were caked with mud and they were clearly still under the impact of the humiliating ordeal they had just experienced. The recent optimism they felt in the truck now completely vanished.

The German sergeant who had stopped them at the first blockade was surprised to see them again. Petka got out of the truck and told him what had happened. "You're lucky to be alive," the sergeant said. "You had the honor of meeting up with the SS's first death squad that began operating in the past few days." He paused for a moment, then added, "Its job is to liquidate leaders, intellectuals, wealthy people, Communists, Jews and the like. If you ask me, I think you're better off returning to Warsaw."

Petka thanked the sergeant and returned to the driver's seat. He turned his head to the rear of the truck. "How are you doing? Can you hold up for a little while longer?" he asked but didn't really expect a response. He knew he had to complete his mission. "In that case, I'm heading now for Lublin, but large military forces have encamped there. From Radzyn Podlaski there's a way leading directly to the river, about thirty-some-odd miles from here. We might run into other blockades, but it's not very likely."

"Is there somewhere we could stop for a few minutes?" Merie asked. "I'm a nurse and I'd like to see if I can be of any help to those who were injured."

"I'll look for a place to stop in the woods, between the trees."

The truck pulled out and picked up speed. Petka took a sharp turn towards Lublin, rocking the passengers, who yelped in pain. "Sorry," Petka shouted, "we have to get out of this area as fast as possible. I'll soon find a place for us to stop for a short rest."

The road curved through the woods and Petka stopped the truck in a clearing, surrounded by tall trees with thick, widespread foliage. Everyone got out, supporting one another, then dropped down on the mud-soaked grass that spread out before them.

Merie's shoulder hurt as was her left hand. Petka pulled out a few old shirts from the front cabin, which she tore into strips and used as a splint for her hand. She then began checking each person's injuries. She began with Radek whose thigh was covered in a large purplish bruise. "There's not much to do with that. It'll hurt you and eventually will get better. You're lucky no bones were broken."

Zosia sat on the grass, withdrawn, hugging her knees. Merie embraced her and whispered, "Where are you hurting, Dear?" Zosia pointed to her right elbow and her ribs. Merie created a sling, which she tied around her neck to support the hand, then turned to the others. They had been beaten, but they seemed able to continue on their journey. "Let's get moving, but if you can, your cargo is sensitive and in pain… so try to avoid quick, sharp turns."

"Are you sure you'll be able to cross the river on the ferry?" Roman asked.

"Look," Petka said, "today, everything's dangerous, and there are no clear rules. You know that since the Ribbentrop-Molotov Pact was signed the Russians and Germans are on good terms… and I heard of people who crossed from the

Russian side over to the German side as well as in the opposite direction. We'll continue on our way and hope for the best."

"Does the fact that my parents live on the Russian side, carry any weight?" Merie asked.

"I hope so," Petka replied.

The rain grew stronger and turned into a storm. As they neared Radzyn, Petka once again bypassed the city, using narrow paths. Finally, he was on the road leading east towards the river. Strong winds rocked the truck and raindrops filtered through the canvas, so Petka slowed down. Again, he hoped that the raging storm would prevent the soldiers at the blockades from coming out to inspect them. This time his prayer was answered. After about an hour and a half on the road, they spotted the large river separating the German and Russian armies and the ferry that connected the two shores.

The ferry was a wide, very long surface that was tied to the east and west banks with a thick metal cable with an engine and a wheel, which pulled it across the river. Vehicles, tractors and wagons filled with farm produce crossed on the ferry, along with many people. Petka stopped his truck behind a line of cars and tractors. They had to undergo inspection at the blockade before getting on the ferry. The truck's passengers were tense and anxiously awaiting the ferry's return from the east bank.

"Everybody out," ordered the sergeant in charge of the blockade. "Have your papers ready." The passengers stepped off the truck, holding their identification papers. The sergeant moved from one to the next, looked at the papers and asked: "Where to?" "Going home," everyone gave the agreed-upon response.

"Are there any soldiers or Jews here?" he asked.

"No. We're students from the other side of the river, we're not Jews," Roman said and they all nodded in agreement.

The wind picked up and the rain turned torrential. The sergeant nodded and let them all get back unto the truck. "Have a safe trip," he said.

The ferry began the process of hooking up to the deck on the west bank. Suddenly, a German staff vehicle pulled up next to the blockade. A German officer stepped out and rushed to the inspection point. He shook off the raindrops that clung to his coat and looked at the row of vehicles waiting to board the ferry. "Did you check them all?" he asked the sergeant.

"Yes, Sir," the sergeant answered. "They're all residents from the other side, returning home."

After the last of the passengers got on the ferry, the operator unhooked it from the deck of the west bank and sailed out.

A field phone rang at the blockade post, on the other end of the line was an officer in charge of the blockade not far from Brest. "Before dawn," he said, "we stopped a truck with six Poles. I instructed them to return to Warsaw, but it's been three hours and the truck still hasn't crossed the blockade at Siedice. If they reach the ferry, they're to be stopped immediately."

The blockade officer glanced at the ferry carrying the six suspects. "No, they haven't come through here," he said.

"You idiot!" he said to the sergeant as he hung up. "You just allowed six people that the Front is looking for, to get on the ferry to the Russian side."

"I hope you'll agree that we never saw them," the sergeant was quick to respond. The officer looked at the ferry as it was being tied up at the east riverbank. Vehicles quickly drove off it, including one pickup truck.

Chapter Five:
The Russian Side Of The Bug River

A Russian soldier instructed everyone to get off the truck and enter the blockade structure. "Take all your stuff with you," he added.

"It looks like the Germans called to say goodbye," the Russian officer said, as he looked at them from behind his table. "Whadda ya say, Vasili, they were beaten up pretty bad, huh?" The soldier nodded.

"What's the purpose of your crossing over to the Russian zone?" the officer asked.

"Officer," Merie said, "I'm a nurse and my parents live in Horodno. I'm on my way to meet them."

"Well, it looks to me, from the beating you got, that the fascists on the other side are not happy about your family reunion," the officer said. "And what about the others?"

"They're students at Warsaw University and they're going back to their families," Petka said. "As for me, I haven't decided yet whether to return to the German side or not. I also have family east of the Bug River."

The officer carefully examined the group before him, while the heavy rain kept hammering outside. He asked them for their ID papers, inspected each one and compared the photo to the person in front of him. "Okay," he said, "these documents aren't valid here. You'll be sent to the NKVD headquarters in Brest, escorted by a soldier who will hold on to your documents. If your stay is approved, you'll be given new documents and you'll be free to continue on your way. Would you like to visit Brest, Vasili?"

"Yes Sir!" Vasili answered.

The officer gave him the documents and Petka got behind the wheel. Vasili sat next to him, holding his gun. Everyone climbed back into the truck and the motor roared. "Well, comrades," Marik suddenly announced, "till now we were Poles under the German occupier and now we're refugees from the German zone." No one said a word.

The winding road to Brest followed the river's course, through the woods. When they reached the outskirts of Brest, Vasili told Petka how to reach the NKVD headquarters stationed in a hotel in the city center. Everyone got off and entered the hotel lobby. Vasili went over to the officer behind a desk, saluted him and said, "I have a group of refugees here," and placed their passports on the table, then saluted once again.

The officer studied the group, opened their passports, compared the photos to the people standing in front of him and said, "First of all, you all have to go through questioning, is there anyone here who speaks Russian?" Merie, Zosia and Petka raised their hands. "The three of you, go over to room number twelve, and the rest to room fourteen. Sit on the benches outside the rooms and wait until your names are called."

When her name was called, Merie opened the door to the room and entered. An officer sitting behind a wooden table told her to sit down facing him and asked in Russian, "Where are you coming from, Mrs. Hackman?"

"From Warsaw," Merie replied. "I'm a registered nurse specializing in children's care. I worked at a hospital. My parents and my brother live in Horodno. I'd like to reunite with my family and get as far away as I can from the Germans, who've occupied Warsaw."

"I see your hand is bandaged," the officer said, "were you injured?"

Merie told him about the encounter with the SS soldiers near the city of Brest. The Russian officer studied her file, then lifted his head and said, "If that's the case, then the SS are nearing Brest. Until now, we heard nothing about that and I thank you for the information. We issue a document to those arriving from the west that confirms their status as refugees from the German zone. Your documents clearly indicate that you were born in this area and you family lives in Horodno, and therefore you will be issued a temporary permit as a Russian citizen that will be attached to your documents. It will allow you to work as a nurse. Welcome to the Russian zone."

"Thank you," Merie said.

"Do you need medical attention?"

"Thank you," Merie smiled, "my hand hurts but I'll be able to take care of it myself."

"Well then, go over to the office next door and they'll give you your permit. After that, you're free to go wherever you please," said the officer.

Merie entered the adjacent office and a few moments later, when she walked out, she met her friends. "I'm on my way to the train station heading home," she said and hugged Zosia and the others. "I wish all of you success in finding your way."

Zosia hugged Merie warmly in return and whispered in her ear, "Thank you for everything. If you find Rafal, give him my regards." Merie smiled and headed confidently towards the exit. From now on, she thought, she's on her own.

Chapter Six: Pinsk

The entrance hall of the train station was teaming with people, most of whom were refugees that had escaped from the German occupation zone and didn't know where they were heading. They were carrying packages that contained the little they were able to retrieve of their possessions. Merie studied the timetable of the outgoing trains. The fragrance of the popular Polish dish, *bigos,* reached her nostrils. It was a hearty stew her mother would cook on winter days, and now she breathed it in and could taste its flavor. She missed her mother so much, longed to embrace her, and her father and, most of all, her brother Gadi.

Merie quickly understood she wouldn't be able to reach Stolin and decided to wait and travel through Pinsk the next day. She could then meet again with friends from the *Tarbut* Gymnasia where she had studied before leaving for nursing school, and stay with the Zlikovitch family in whose home she lived for five years during her years as a student. That high-school, which was part of a network of the *Tarbut* Hebrew education system, had opened four years before Merie joined and quickly accredited as the finest high-school in the region. It boasted state-of-the-art physics, chemistry and natural science labs. But its uniqueness lay in the fact that all studies were conducted in Hebrew. All the teachers spoke Hebrew. Not the archaic Hebrew taught in the *Heder*, the religious elementary schools, but the new, modern language spoken in *Eretz Yisrael*.

Meir Zlikovitch was a wood trader and was a friend of her father, Ephraim, who specialized in forest management and assessed the value of wood put up for tenders. Meir was of a Zionist leaning and introduced her family to the *Tarbut* Gymnasia in Pinsk. He convinced her parents to enroll her there despite the high tuition fees. He invited her to stay in his home during her studies, and thus Merie became part of the Zlikovitch family.

The train pulled into the Brest station, whistling and puffing. Although the cars were already packed, many others pushed their way into the train. Merie squeezed through the crowds until she reached the last car of the train. Its door was shut but she forced it open and rushed inside just as the train whistle blew and the doors closed. You can survive a war only if you keep moving, she thought, as she sat on the floor, pulling her knees close to her chin and hugging her knapsack. The train's swaying movement soon had her drop off and she fell asleep.

When the train came to a shrieking stop, Merie woke up and looked out at the city of Kobryn. The journey to Pinsk was still long, but her stomach cramped. Hunger. She realized that since leaving Warsaw she hadn't eaten anything. But she had to wait as the train continued its long journey until finally reaching Pinsk's outskirts. Merie recalled her life in Pinsk, which, for a young girl arriving from a small town at the time, seemed to her a metropolis. She wondered who from the Gymnasia's graduates stayed there while she left the school and the youth movement at the end of the eleventh grade and never got her graduation insignia.

The train came to a full stop and Merie rushed out to the platform. She bought herself a large, sliced sausage meat sandwich and a cold drink at the food stall, then sat on a bench at the edge of the platform to have it in peace. Gradually, she felt her strength returning.

The drizzling rain gave way to snowflakes, which began to fall and cover the streets. Merie quickened her steps to the Zlikovitch house near the river. As she approached, she noticed its gate was sealed with a chain. "Do you know the Zlikovitch family that lives here?" she asked a passerby who looked to be Jewish.

"Certainly. The family left for *Eretz Yisrael* two years ago."

Merie thanked him and headed for the Gymnasia building that was just a block away. Its gate was open, as was the front door. The building was empty, there was no one around. Suddenly she heard footsteps behind her, turning around she saw Mark, the gatekeeper and superintendent.

"Hello Mark, do you remember me?"

"I certainly do, Merie. You left in the eleventh grade, didn't you? As you see, the *Tarbut* Gymnasia is no longer, there're no students, no teachers. The Russians instated the Yevsektsiya..."

Merie nodded, she was familiar with that term from Rafal's stories. The Yevsektsiya was the Jewish section of the Soviet Communist Party that opposed Zionism and the Hebrew language. They believed that Zionism represented the Jewish bourgeoisie.

"We explained to them that Hebrew is our culture. But they approved only Russian and Yiddish. If we'd been willing to teach in Yiddish," Mark added, "and break all connection with *Eretz Yisrael*, they would have let us continue, but it would've no longer been the *Tarbut* Gymnasia. Without Hebrew, the *Tarbut* Gymnasia would be irrelevant."

"So what now?" Merie asked.

"Meanwhile, I'm watching over the building. Waiting for the Yevsektsiya people to come and take it over. Maybe they'll turn it into a club or another school. Who knows."

"And what about the kids from the *Hashomer Hatzair* movement?" Merie asked and felt a stab to her heart. "Do you know if they're still meeting at the Nest?"

"All I know is that they stopped holding activities at the Nest," Mark replied. "I suggest you talk to Shoshana. Remember her? She was in the school's PTA and the youth movement's parents' committee. I think she'll be able to fill you in."

"Can I just look around the building a little?" she asked.

"Suit yourself," Mark said.

Merie entered one of the classrooms and shut her eyes. She could hear the students' clamor during recess, the melody of the Hebrew language that was so different from Polish. How much fun it was to gossip with her girlfriends in a language that no one outside the school or the youth movement understood. A wave of deep longing for those days, never to return, swept over her. Tears filled her eyes and trickled down her face. Mark was looking at her. She wiped away her tears and smiled. "Thank you," she said and walked out.

The gentle touch of the snow was delightful as she made her way to The Blecher house where Shoshana's family lived. She knew Shoshana well, from the days when she and Shoshana's daughter, Batya, were close friends in school. Merie rang the bell and the door opened. "Merie?" What... what are you doing here?" Shoshana gazed at her surprised.

"Aren't you going to let me in first?" Merie said, smiling.

Shoshana hugged her closely and opened the door wide.

The house was warm and inviting, and a whiff of food cooking in the kitchen filled the air. Shoshana invited her to remove her coat and sit down as she put a large bowl of beet soup before her with its deep flavor enriched from marrow-filled soup bones.

"Where's Batya? Is she still in Pinsk?"

"Batya left a few years ago to *Eretz Yisrael* and last year, with good *mazal*, she got married and lives in Tel-Aviv."

"I didn't know... the last few years, the hospital was my entire world."

"Merie, I want you to eat, and then tell me everything you've been through. Then you'll take a bath and, of course, you'll stay here, no arguments."

Merie savored the soup and told Shoshana everything. Hearing her story, Shoshana wrung her hands, then turned to the stove and brought her a dishful of hot stew and roasted potatoes. A pleasant weakness washed over her. Someone else was taking charge. She finished her meal and stretched out.

"Now, a bath. Do you have a change of clothes?" Shoshana asked, not waiting for an answer.

She took out clean underwear, a shirt and a pair of pants from the closet and handed them to Merie. Then she filled the bath with hot water and as Merie sank in the warm water that cradled her, she closed her eyes and felt as if she were floating inside a womb. Thirty minutes later a knock on the door shook her awake. The water had turned cold so she got out, got dressed and went into the dining room to join Shoshana and her husband, Zalman.

"Hello, Merie, Batya's dear friend," Zalman said.

"Hello, Zalman," Merie answered.

Merie sat down to talk with them. "So," she began, "how are you? And where is Yecheskel and..."

"I see you don't know about Yecheskel... he immigrated to Palestine and was murdered by Arab rioters."

Merie looked at them and a shudder ran up her spine. "Yecheskel? How did that happen?" she asked.

"What we were told is that he joined the *Notrim*, he was a guard with the Jewish auxiliary unit of the British Mandate police. The British gave them weapons to protect the roads from Arab snipers or gangs. One morning, about a year ago, before Batya's wedding, while on their way to opening the road to

Haifa a sniper shot and killed him." Shoshana's eyes filled with tears. "I have no words to tell you what I've been through..." Merie went over to her and embraced her. "I was sure," Shoshana added, "that Yecheskel would be safer in Palestine than here, but look how he was taken from us. Who can say that Pinsk is a safer place? Is there any place safe today?"

"You certainly can feel proud of him and the path he chose. Yecheskel lost his life protecting Jews, holding a weapon in his hand. There is no one to protect the Jews in Warsaw. I think that if life has any meaning, then the way one dies also has meaning..."

"For us, there's no comfort in that," Shoshana said.

Silence filled the room.

"So what happened with Batya's wedding?" Merie asked.

"Weddings should not be postponed. We waited until the *shiva* [the traditional seven days of mourning] ended, and the wedding took place a month later. Right after that, we returned to Pinsk."

"And what's become of the *Hashomer Hatzair* movement?" Merie asked, trying to divert Shoshana from her grief.

"Not much. Actually, the movement's center, the Nest, no longer exists," Shoshana said, sniffling. "The decision was made to shut it down. I organize the movement's members and counselors that escaped from the occupied zone. Zalman and I help them as best we can."

"A week ago," Zalman offered, "we held a meeting of the movement's graduates. Nine of them decided to try to cross the border to Lithuania. From there, they'll try to reach *Eretz Yisrael*. Others decided to go south to Rovno, where veteran movement members from nests in White Russia and the Ukraine are gathering. We think they are planning to reach Romania and board an illegal ship heading for *Eretz Yisrael*, or Turkey."

Merie looked at them fondly. "I'm going to visit my parents and then I'll also be going to Rovno," she said. "Meanwhile, let me tell you that I too got married."

Shoshana stood up and hugged her. "*Mazal tov*, Merie. Who's the lucky guy?"

"His name is Rafal, Rafael in Hebrew. He has a Ph.D. in history from Warsaw University. He escaped before me... I don't know where he is. But there's a chance that he too is in Rovno. Shoshana, Pinsk is just over a hundred and twenty miles from Brest. You must leave, go to *Eretz Yisrael*, to Romania or into the Russian areas. I believe that sooner or later the Nazis will invade here too. Don't be fooled, these aren't the Germans who occupied Pinsk in World War I. I saw for myself what they are capable of."

Shoshana gave her a tired look. "No place is safe for the Jews," she said.

Chapter Seven:
Going Home

Before the sun came up, Merie entered the kitchen, where she found Shoshana sitting at the table, sipping a cup of coffee.

"Come, sit down," Shoshana said, "I'll fix you a light breakfast."

Merie took her seat at the table and sipped her coffee. Shoshana handed her a thick slice of rye bread spread with a generous layer of yellow butter.

"Have you thought about the conversation we had last night?" Merie asked.

"Of course, we have discussed leaving Pinsk before you came. We wanted to be with Batya and close to Yecheskel's grave."

"I'll be glad to know that you have left. I'm worried about you. I'll never forget the two of you and the way you made me feel, so welcome. I'm going to catch the next bus out to Stolin and from there to Horodno. I miss my parents so much."

"Give them our warmest regards."

"I will," Merie said, "and, please, take care of yourselves."

The sun was shining and the sky was blue, but the air was chilly and the streets were covered with a thin layer of ice. As Merie walked towards the bus station, she recalled the winters when the river froze and they would all go ice-skating on it. That was her favorite sport during her years at the Gymnasia.

The train station was packed with people rushing from one end to the other. Merie bought a bus ticket to Stolin, there she would have to find a way to reach Horodno, which, though considered a precinct of Stolin, was far from the city.

She got on a rickety old bus that was jammed with people, and found a seat on the back bench, next to a farmer who was on his way back from the market. He was holding a net cage, in which a noisy hen kept cackling. The bus finally pulled out, gasping and heaving and Merie gazed out the window as Pinsk drew further away. She shut her eyes and thought about Rafal. Their last meeting was so brief. She was worried lest he be sent to a labor camp in Siberia. She had heard of the horrors there. Maybe he went to her parents' home? No. Rafal wouldn't go there without her. After they were married, they went to meet her parents. Rafal and Merie's father hit it off immediately as they both loved history. Though Rafal was considered a brilliant student in the Polish academy, he kept his distance from the Jewish surroundings and did not accept the Zionist ideal, nor did he support the establishment of a Jewish homeland in Eretz Yisrael. He was a Communist and spoke very little Hebrew, which he had learned as a child in Heder.

After a three-hour ride, the bus reached Stolin and stopped in the city center. Merie got off at the market square and walked over to the horse-and-buggy station. "How much is it to Horodno?" she asked the buggy-driver perched on his seat.

"I don't reach Horodno, but try the driver next to me," he pointed to another buggy-driver. "He lives there and he'll be glad to take you."

Merie went over to the other driver and asked if he could take her to Horodno.

"Mrs. Hackman, don't you remember me?" He asked.

Merie looked at him more closely. It was Yurek. She remembered him as a cross-eyed young boy from their childhood years. "Of course I remember!"

Yurek smiled. "I'm heading for Horodno in fifteen minutes with two passengers. The ride costs one zloty."

"Terrific," she replied, "save me the best seat. I'm going over to get something to eat and will be back in a jiffy."

Merie bought herself a sandwich and a drink and paid him one zloty. Everything costs one zloty, she thought. Suddenly, she spotted her parents' neighbors, Vera and Yechiel.

"Hello," she said, this time in Yiddish.

"Hello, Merie!" said Eva in sheer surprise. "I'm so happy to see you! Your parents brag about you all the time. Godel and your father miss you so much, and they're worried about you..."

"Did you just arrive unexpectedly?" Yechiel asked. "Your father didn't mention anything about your coming."

"Yes, just a few days ago I was still working at a hospital as a nurse."

"You're going with Yurek?" Vera asked.

"Yes," Merie replied. "I don't know of any other way to get to Horodno..."

"For sure," Yechiel chuckled, "just a horse and buggy. Actually there a few pickup trucks, but we and your dad do just fine with the horse and buggy."

"My dad was always conservative," Merie smiled. "He said that horses rarely break down."

"Your brother was very lucky to finish his studies, with honors at that, at the Gymnasia in Pinsk before the Russians entered," Vera said. "And he's grown so tall in the past year."

"Are you coming?" Yurek called out.

They climbed into the buggy, pulled by two brown horses. Yurek spurred the horses on with his whip and they dashed on their way. After a short ride, they turned into a path leading to the dense forest. Thick raspberry bushes stood tall at the entrance, preventing easy access. "The forest is a loving shelter for those who are familiar with it and its paths, and a cruel rival for those who don't know its secrets," Merie whispered to herself the words her father often said. Her heart was pounding as she drew closer to home.

Merie longed to see her mother's face and feel her closeness. She knocked lightly on the door. Her mother, Minna, opened the door and her eyes lit up.

"Efraim!" Minna shouted and rushed to embrace Merie. "Look who's here!"

Her father came to the door. He was somewhat bent and his hair had grown thinner. Merie spread her arms out to them and fell into their hug. "We were so worried," Minna said and wiped a tear from her eyes, while Merie too teared up.

"Where's Gadi?" She asked, and there he was, coming towards her with his arms outstretched pulling her away from her parents' embrace, and asked, "How're you doing, Sis?"

Merie smiled at him. "You've grown!" she said, gazing at this tall, slim young man whose rich brown hair fell in thick curly locks on his forehead, as was the fashion among the young men in Pinsk. She rested her head on his chest, against his heart that she knew so well.

They sat down in the kitchen. Minna prepared coffee with milk for everyone, as Merie glanced around the house she had grown up in. Signs of aging were everywhere.

"Where is Rafal?" Minna asked.

"Things got tough and he left you?" Efraim asked.

"No, Father," Merie answered, "I asked him to get away."

"A husband's duty is to stay with his wife and support her. If not, what did you get married for? And why didn't he wait for you here?"

"The worst thing, believe me, is not the battles and the bombings of Warsaw, but the German occupation that followed. They began abusing the Jews from the very first day, and no one dared to come to their help. I saw with my own eyes how German soldiers ripped the beard off the face of an old man."

No one spoke. Efraim nodded from side to side, finding it hard to believe. "I'm sure those soldiers will be punished," he said. "I know the Germans. I used to trade with them in wood. They were always fair with me."

Merie looked at him and let out a sigh. "During the Great War," Efraim continued, ignoring her response, "I was a soldier in the Russian army and when I was caught and sent to a POW camp, the Germans treated us fairly."

"I know you it's hard for you to believe what I'm saying, Father, but these aren't the same Germans you knew," Merie said. "These are Nazis, there's nothing fair or decent about them, they hate us, they're anti-Semitic. Believe me, the officer in charge of these soldiers could have commanded them to stop, but he stood there and enjoyed watching their cruelty."

"You must be hungry," Minna said. "There's kugel and meat dumplings."

Tears flowed from Merie's eyes. "If you only knew how much I longed to eat your food, Mother..."

"So, Sis, tell us, how did you escape?" Gadi asked.

"That's enough for now," Minna intervened. "There'll be plenty of time for stories. Go wash your hands and come to eat."

Merie looked at her parents. How naïve they are, she thought, and how easily they can be hurt.

Chapter Eight: Horodno

Six days had passed since Merie returned to her parents' home. The home-cooked meals and the warmth of her close family did her good and overpowered the images she carried of the war and the occupation.

Before the Friday evening Shabbat meal, Merie and her father went for a walk in the woods near to their home. "The mud is boggy because of the peat and there aren't many paths we can walk on that aren't dangerous. I hope you remember everything I taught you about the woods. Do you still love the sweet berries?"

Merie smiled. "Father, you've been repeating that warning ever since I was born. My senses have grown sharper, and thanks to them, I succeeded in escaping from Warsaw. Now let's go looking for wild berries."

"You know, sometimes when I go walking in the woods, I remember how you stood up to the leader of the Patlora gang, and you were only four years old. Back then, at the end of the Great War, we escaped to the woods many times. The Poles fought the Russians, then the Ukrainian gangs, the Patlora, arrived and fought the two armies. What they really wanted was to rob the Jews and kill them."

"Probably because the Jews, at least some of them, had possessions that could be stolen. What could they steal from the poor villagers?" Merie asked.

"That's your husband's influence on you. The Jews were always the outsiders who could be blamed for everything, therefore it was easier to attack them," Efraim said. "Anyway, in that particular case, a short time after I returned from the German POW camp, we learned that a Ukrainian gang was heading here so all the town's residents fled to the forest. We later learned that the person who led them was a Ukrainian who knew the forest paths well. So there we were, gathered closely on one of the forest's clearings and waiting in absolute silence, when suddenly we're surrounded by Ukrainians on horseback. When the Ukrainian commander asked who's in charge, everyone pointed to me, perhaps because I had served in the army, I'm not sure."

Merie nodded. She knew that story well. She had heard it many times.

"'You, come with us and show us where your monies are hidden,' the commander said. 'If we don't find the money, we'll kill you before we leave.' Then, all of a sudden, to my surprise, and everyone's surprise for that matter, you stood in front of his horse and yelled, 'You won't take my father! You won't take my father!' The commander was stunned. He grabbed you by your dress and sat you on his horse, facing him. Mother shouted out, 'Please, put my daughter down,' but the commander raised his hand and shouted, 'Silence!' Everyone fell silent and then he turned to you and asked, 'How old are you, little girl?' and you said, 'I'm four years old.' Then he asked, 'And who is your father?' And you pointed at me. 'And why do you think I can't take your father?' He asked. You looked directly at him and said, 'Because I don't allow it.' He smiled at you and then put you down right into Mother's arms and said, 'Well, alright. If she doesn't allow me, I can't take her father.' He turned his horse around, signaled to his soldiers, and within minutes we found ourselves alone in the forest. Your courage and determination amazed every single one there. As you see, even at the age of four you were the topic of discussion."

"Father, two days from now I'll be going to Rovno to try and get a job at the hospital there and see if I can find Rafal."

"Why not stay with us a bit longer till you're healed? What's the rush?"

Merie hesitated briefly. "I figure the Germans will be invading here as well. Nazism and Communism are so contradictory to one another that there's no way they can share a common border. Horodno is about 125 miles from the border, which means you're exposed. Gadi graduated, he has a matriculation diploma in Hebrew, he's a brilliant student and a gifted violin player, yet he won't be able to study at the university here, or in any university throughout Europe. Father, the best and safest place for him is Eretz Yisrael. I'm going to Rovno to find ways to make Aliyah, to reach Eretz Yisrael. Gadi can then try to get into the Technion and be certified."

"Talk to him," Efraim said, "if he agrees, we won't stand in his way."

"And what about you two?" Merie asked. "I'd be much happier to know that you're in Rovno, at least. Mother has cousins there who also deal in wood and you won't have any trouble getting work. But mainly, you'll be much farther away from the border."

"Your mother and I are staying here, in our home. I'm not willing to become a refugee." The air was chilly and a wind began to blow through the trees. "It's getting late. Our Shabbat meal is probably waiting for us. I don't want your mother to worry."

"What did the two of you talk about for so long?" Gadi asked when they returned. "Mother almost sent me out to look for you."

Merie washed her hands and sat down at the table. "Godel, Sir, after dinner could we perhaps be treated to a violin recital?"

"I haven't played the violin seriously for the past six months," Gadi replied, "but I'll be glad to play a few Tchaikovsky melodies."

"Great," Merie said, "but before that, I want to talk to you."

"About what?" Minna asked.

"A brother-sister thing," Merie replied.

After dinner, Gadi took up his violin and played the second movement of Tchaikovsky's violin concerto and then added a short piece by the Polish composer, Wieniawski. After that, the two siblings went into Gadi's room. He stretched down on his bed and Merie took a seat facing him.

"What are you planning to do, Gadi?" She asked.

"Merie, I'm devastated by what's happening. Forgive me if I'm not overly concerned about where I'll study or play violin."

"Listen, my dear brother, I stayed overnight at Shoshana's home in Pinsk. She told me that all the Movement's counselors and graduates in Rovno are looking for a way to make Aliyah to Eretz Yisrael, legal or otherwise. For you, it's the ideal solution."

Gadi looked at her fondly. "Why do you want to arrange everyone's life?" He asked. "And what about your life?"

"I'm preoccupied with my life and I'm trying to digest the whole situation. I want you to come with me to Rovno and check out the possibility of immigrating to Eretz Yisrael. I spoke to Father about it and he gives his blessing."

"But I don't want to," Gadi said.

"Gudel, what's left here for you?"

"As long as Mother and Father are here, I'm staying with them."

"But you don't get it, the war is about to break."

"Merie, you have a husband you need to track down. I'll stay with our parents and hope for the best."

Merie had hoped she'd be able to get her message across to her family, but she failed. She went to her room, undressed and got in bed. Under the heavy covers, she cried over her future and the future of her family, as if sensing what was about to transpire.

Chapter Nine: Rovno

The forest seemed to follow its own timetable, detached from the humans who were running their wars. It was freezing cold outside, the temperature dropped to below zero. Merie dressed warmly and covered her face and nose with a thick woolen scarf. That morning, she was in tears as she said goodbye, leaving of her parents. Her father embraced her long and close and his kind, brown eyes wordlessly begged her to take care of herself. Her mother stroked her cheek gently and asked that she stay in touch as best she could. Most difficult for her was parting from Gadi. She didn't know if she would ever see her family again, but now she had to focus on her goal: Find a job and look for Rafal. She missed him so much. He was always the one who knew what should be done. She hoped he would be in Rovno.

The train ride from Pinsk reminded her that the world was on the brink of war. The crowded cars were filled with tired, tattered refugees drifting from place to place. Merie found a spot where she sat in a corner near one of the car doors. She held a note with the address of relatives who lived in Rovno in an expansive apartment on a major boulevard, reminiscent of Warsaw. The train car was stuffy and suffocating, the air permeated with the sour smell of sweat. Passengers kept moving about restlessly as if searching for a safe place .

When the train pulled into the station at Rovno, Merie got out and sighed with relief. The knapsack on her shoulder was stuffed full. She wondered for a moment where to head first, but her eyes suddenly caught sight of Minna and Aaron at the end of the platform. They were friends from the Movement's nest in Pinsk. They were wearing high shoes and thick coats and were carrying very large knapsacks. Merie called out to them and they came towards her.

"Minna! What are you two doing here, dressed like mountain climbers?" She laughed.

Minna glanced around her then pulled Merie into a quiet corner. "We heard that the Mossad Le'Aliya Bet, which is organizing clandestine immigration to Palestine, opened a camp in Romania for young Poles who are waiting to board a ship to Eretz Yisrael. Our cover story is that we're on our way to a trek in the Tatra Mountains and that we got lost."

Merie chuckled. "Just a few days ago I managed to cross the border from the German side to the Russian side and we were caught. We were beaten up."

"Oh, wow," Minna said. "So what are you doing in Rovno?"

"I want to see if I can work here in the Jewish Hospital. I wish you two the best of luck," she added. "Stay safe."

Merie decided to begin by checking out the hospital.

In the hospital's main lobby Merie saw a sign, 'Head Nurse,' and knocked on the door, then opened it slightly and was amazed to see, sitting behind a desk wearing a white uniform and apron, her friend Magda Yachimovitz, her old-time classmate from the Nursing School in Warsaw.

"Magda!" Merie burst out in unrestrained laughter.

"Merie!" Magda shouted and they fell into each other's arms.

"I came here from Pinsk to see if I could get a job at the hospital," Merie explained.

"Perfect timing!" Magda said. "The nurses here were trained in peripheral Russian hospitals and I'm dying for some who studied in Warsaw. I'm ready to take a certified nurse like you right now. And if you need a place to stay, I'll try to arrange for you to get a room in one of the hospital-owned apartments."

"Thank you, Magda. But I'm going to search for my husband and if I find him, I'll want to be with him."

"But of course!" Magda replied. "Tell me everything, what happened and how come you're alone." So Merie told her all that had happened.

"If I understand correctly the situation today," Magda said, "I think you'll find Rafal very soon. It's just amazing, isn't it, how we've just gotten an excellent nurse! I'll place you in the emergency room. This is a small hospital and the children's and adults' wards are combined, but I'm sure you know how to take care of everyone."

"For sure," Merie replied.

"Come with me," Magda said as she stood up. "Let's get you processed at the personnel office." She hugged Merie once more. "I'm so thrilled you're here," she added.

The two Nursing School friends walked out of the office with their arms around each other and headed to the administration office. Magda apologized that she had to hurry on to a staff meeting and Merie stayed back to fill out the required forms.

As she headed for the central city square, she thought about Magda and how lucky she was. Suddenly, she spotted a familiar face. Could it be? Was she dreaming? She shut her eyes and opened them again. She felt her heart pounding. A yell escaped her lips and she ran straight into Rafal's ardent embrace.

2.

THE ESCAPE
TO TASHKENT, 1941

Chapter One:
Spring In Rovno

After a harsh winter, springtime came to Rovno and the city was bursting with a colorful rainbow of blooming flowers and the green foliage of the trees.

Merie and Rafal lived in a small two-room apartment allocated to them by the hospital, and Merie was very happy and doing great in the hospital. Contrary to her early worries, the Germans had targeted all their efforts to Western Europe. Firstly to Norway, then to Denmark, Holland, Belgium and France. The last month of May, Hitler had suddenly turned his forces to attacking Serbia and Greece, adding them to his conquests. The whole of Europe, from the Bug River in the east, to the Atlantic Ocean in the west, was under Nazi regime.

Soon after arriving in Rovno, Merie became pregnant but miscarried in her third month. Several months later, she again got pregnant and in mid-March of 1941, their son Alfred, was born. They nicknamed him Alec. As her job at the hospital emergency room was assured, she could devote herself to caring for her son. Rafal was well connected with the leadership of the Communist Party in Rovno whose members were mostly Jews. As an expert in organizing archives, Rafal found a position with the Russian military archives in Rovno.

Rovno was a bustling junction of communication networks and train lines, and served as the Regional and main Headquarters of the Fifth Red Banner Army. It was Rafal's job to organize the HQ archives from the ground up, and his extensive experience served well his Russian army employers.

While Rafal was busy with the Communist Party's issues, Merie continued her work at the hospital and met with her longtime friends from the Hashomer Hatzair movement in Rovno. The escape route to Romania has been blocked and those who remained behind in the refugee camp near the Danube River, began losing their patience, feeling abandoned. So some considered crossing the border over to the Russian occupation zones even at the risk of being caught, imprisoned or even expelled to the Siberian labor camps.

Merie was holding Alec in her arms, gently patting his back after being nursed, when she heard a knock on the door. Opening the door there stood Gadi, smiling his bright smile with his arms stretched out. Both Merie and Alec were enveloped in his arms.

"Gadi! What in the...? For months I've been contemplating of taking Alec to Horodno to visit our parents, but he's been sick quite a bit, you know, fever and colds again and again, and now, you're here!"

"Can't I visit my sister and my very first nephew?"

"Come in, come in," Merie quickly said.

"He looks just like you!" Gadi said and took his knapsack of his shoulder. "Just so you know, Mother and Father wanted to come with me, but Father having back pains was concerned about the long train ride, and Mother, well, you know her, she won't leave him. Okay, now let me hold my nephew." Gadi cuddled Alec in his arms and the baby smiled at him. "See that? He already loves his uncle."

"Let's go for a walk in the park," Merie suggested. "It's a lovely day outside." Gadi nodded and Merie quickly changed Alec, dressed him warmly for the outing.

"Hold on," Gadi said and opened his knapsack. "Mother knitted something special for him." He pulled out a knitted blue overall and handed it to Merie. She hugged it to her and sniffed its fragrance.

"Let's go," Gadi said.

"Wait," Merie hesitated, "I want to put his grandma's gift on him." They all went down to the park.

"Rafal!" she cried as she stepped out to the street. "What are you doing home at this hour?"

"Hello Gudel!" Rafal said as his face lit up. "I came to take a change of clothes. We've been put on alert and will have to stay in the archives for several nights. So sorry, Gudel, I'm going to be away for the next few days. Will you be staying with us for a while?"

"I'm afraid I'll be heading back to Pinsk this evening," Gadi answered.

"This evening?" Merie asked. "Why don't you stay here? You might even find a job."

"I'll say goodbye," Rafal bent to kiss Merie and Alec. "Stay well, Gadi."

Merie and Gadi entered the park and found a bench next to the water fountain. Alec was asleep in his baby carriage and all was quiet and calm.

"What are you planning to do, Gudel? It has been a year and a half since I visited Horodno. What's changed?"

"I might be able to get a job at the plywood factory in town. I don't see any other options to earn money in the present situation."

"You know, Gudel," Merie began, "if war breaks out, I'm going to take Alec and escape."

Gadi sighed. "Mother and Father won't leave Horodno. They'll wait and see how things develop and then decide what to do. I'll stay with them and hope that everything will be okay." He was silent for a moment and then smiled and said, "Tell me, why are we talking about war? Just look at the weather, it's a wonderful spring day, the sun is warm and pleasant, lovely little Alec is sleeping peacefully. Everything's good."

Just then Merie noticed her friend Etka, from the Hashomer youth movement. She waved to her and Etka came towards them. "You don't have to wave, I spotted you from the road, sitting here on the bench. And who's the young man with you?"

"This is my brother, Gadi."

Etka shook his hand and sat down next to them. "Did you also study at the *Tarbut* Gymnasia in Pinsk?" she asked.

"Yes I did," Gadi answered, "and I was also in the Hashomer movement and during my last two years at school I was a counselor. But it's fallen apart ever since the Russians came in."

"Same thing happened here in Rovno," Etka said. "Merie, I'm glad I ran into you. I wanted to say goodbye, we're leaving for Tashkent."

"Who is going and why to Tashkent?" Merie asked.

"There's a group of us, graduates of the Movement. We've got nothing to look for here. Tashkent is close to the Iranian border and I know that a lot of our friends continued on to Palestine from there." Etka stood up, gave Merie a hug, then bent over the carriage and lightly placed a kiss on Alec's forehead.

"Give our friends my regards. Perhaps one day we'll meet in Tashkent or Palestine," Merie said.

Etka shook Gadi's hands. "You're invited to come along," she said. "Handsome men like you are always welcome in our group or in a kibbutz in Palestine." She then turned around and walked quickly out of the park.

"I have to go, I have to catch my train," Gadi said. "I'm so happy I got to see you and little Alec. When he wakes up, give him a kiss from me, and from his grandparents too, and most important, take care of yourself, these are difficult times for raising a child."

Merie watched him as he walked away, not realizing she would never see him again.

Chapter Two: War

Alec's crying woke Merie up. She glanced at the clock. It was three-thirty in the morning. She stretched her hand groping for Rafal, but then remembered he had stayed the night at the Archives to work. A light rain tapped on the windowpane as she lifted Alec up and nursed him.

An annoying noise was continually heard throughout the dark night sounding like a thunderstorm. Merie went over to the kitchen window and peered outside. She tried to better understand what was going on, and then shuddering she realized that what she was hearing was the thunder of canons.

The German invasion of the Russian zone had begun. 'What I imagined is now happening,' she thought to herself. The things Rafal said the other day, the fact that he had to remain at work all night, and now the canons' roar added up to one unavoidable truth.

Merie was afraid. She is responsible not just for herself now, but also for her three-month-old son. What is she to do? Why is Rafal always absent from the crucial junctions of her life? She returned Alec to his crib. Covered in sweat, she filled a glass of water and slowly sipped it. She shut the window and made herself a cup of coffee, sat down, breathing heavily. She tried to decide what she would have to do in the next few days. The Germans will reach Rovno in no time, which means she has to get away as far as possible. But what about Rafal? No, she must save her son, she must escape from the inferno.

Merie stood up, filled with determination, and looked for a suitcase. She planned what food items she had to take with her.

The grocery store at the corner will open at seven-thirty so then she'll buy all she'll need for them to survive for the next few days.

Daybreak came and Merie woke up Alec, changed him and tied him to her with a bed sheet. She put on a raincoat and went out. Very few people were out and about. She entered the grocery store and asked for bread, hard cheese, and a long, dry salami.

"Five cans of condensed milk, please, and three packages of sweet biscuits." The grocer gave her a suspicious look. She knew that by the end of the day, everybody would have realized that war has begun and by then it would be impossible to get anything at all. If Rafal doesn't return by twelve noon, she would take Alec to the train station and look for a train heading east, to Kiev or any other eastern city.

Back home, Merie placed Alec in his crib, then she took down her old knapsack and Rafal's one as well. She packed both with just the most necessary items, took out their two heavy coats from the closet, and warm boots, and placed them next to the knapsacks. Though the weather wasn't cold, she knew that without these items, they wouldn't survive the freezing Russian winter. Then she sat down waiting for Rafal. Meanwhile, she picked up Alec and began nursing him, so that he wouldn't be hungry when they left.

Rafal arrived home at noon and seemed pale. "What's all this?" he asked upon seeing the knapsacks and coats. "We have to go east," Merie said, "as far away as we can. When I got up at three-thirty this morning, I heard the thundering of the canons from the west."

"You're right," Rafal said. "You understood what the entire Russian leadership understood only thirty minutes ago. Moscow gave orders not to return fire so as not to give the Germans an excuse to attack. But now the order has changed to return fire, but the Germans are moving forward at top speed. We have to clear the Army's archives to Kiev and its headquarters as well. A military train will be leaving in the early evening to Kiev, and the Archives have been allocated the last three train cars. The colonel approved my bringing you and Alec on the train with me. Once we're in Kiev, we'll manage."

"We won't stay in Kiev. We'll keep moving eastward."

"Merie... I'm not a Russian citizen and I don't have to enlist, but the Archives people rely on me."

"I will not stay in Kiev!" Merie shouted. "And I'll do it with or without you. My responsibility is towards our child and I will make sure he's got a chance to live!"

Rafal sat down at the kitchen table and didn't answer. After a short pause, he said, "Merie, ever since my high-school days, I've been a Communist and a Marxist, but I'm not stupid or blind. The Communist regime is a terrorist regime. Sometimes, terrorism has its own logic, and though I don't agree with its ways and methods, I can understand its motives. But mostly, terror's objective is simply terror, in order to instill fear and gain power and control. We are guests in this country. My papers indicate I'm a refugee from the German-occupied zone. At any moment, I could be arrested as a spy and discover that the secret police can put a bullet through my head faster than they drink a shot of vodka! And, by the way, they'd shoot you just a quickly. As to our son, I don't even want to think about it.

So we must get as far away from the western German border as quickly as possible. It'll take time until the Russian army is able to halt the Germans' advance. And remember, we have no control over our fate. If we want to survive, we must try to remain unobtrusive and avoid any confrontation with the authorities. Right now, the colonel at the Archives needs me."

Merie was flabbergasted. Never before had she had such an open, straightforward discussion with Rafal. "So what now?"

"I'm going back to the Archives. When I return, be ready to leave. I'm glad you packed already." Rafal stood up slowly, leaned over the crib and kissed Alec's forehead, then embraced Merie and kissed her.

Merie was left alone in the apartment, with Alec and with her fears. Suddenly, she heard a sound that was familiar to her from Warsaw during the bombardment. She hurried over to the window and opened it. Black planes flying beneath the clouds were approaching. Merie heard the bombs bursting. She grabbed Alec and rushed to the basement. She wasn't alone, another twenty or so tenants were crowded together there, fearful and anxious. In one single swoop, their lives had changed. No matter what the outcome of the war would be, they were now facing the unknown, which looked bitter and bad.

Every once in a while, the apartment building shook with the bombs' shock waves, but the attack was not on the city. Nearly an hour later, she returned to her apartment. She opened the window and saw black smoke rising from the Rovno train station. Apparently, the attack was directed there as well as at the military airport. She realized how lucky she was that she didn't go with Alec to the train station. All she could do now was wait for Rafal. She sat down on the couch and looked around her at all the things they had purchased in the past year-and-a-half. Leaving their home will be the second time she had to abandon her home, this time for good. She longed for some stability, for a place where she could live with her husband and raise her child without fearing for their lives.

Merie's thoughts were interrupted by the sound of the front door opening. Rafal shut the door behind him. He looked exhausted. "I was worried about you," he said. "There was an air attack on the airport and train station. Most of the terminal building was destroyed, and by a miracle most of the train tracks remained intact." Merie stayed silent gazing at him. "Our train will leave at 2:30 a.m. from platform number five. I have transfer papers for all three of us. But there's a slight change in plans, Merie. The archives are being sent out in two trains and the Colonel insists that I leave with the second. I asked that you and Alec be seated on the first train. Who knows what'll happen tomorrow..."

"I don't want to go alone again," Merie said, "I want you to be with me."

"I'll be just a few hours behind you. My train will be leaving tomorrow morning at 8:30. Sweetheart, I'm certain that we'll meet in Kiev and continue from there together. But please, when you reach Kiev, take a hotel room near the train station and wait for me at the station's entrance tomorrow between twelve noon and two o'clock. If I don't show up in three days, go on east." They held each other tight and Merie shivered in his arms. "I know, Sweetheart," Rafal said, "but I have no choice." Merie couldn't stop her tears, helpless and anxious. Rafal stroked her hair, and then Alec woke up. Merie quickly wiped away her tears. "We forgot there's someone else here who needs our attention...," she said and picked up Alec, who needed a diaper change. "Come on, let's bathe you," she said. "I don't know when we will have another opportunity I'm so glad that yesterday I had the chance to say goodbye to Gudel," she said, and gently placed Alec into the sheet tied around her shoulder. She buttoned her coat up covering the infant, put a woolen cap on his head and shouldered her knapsack. Before shutting the door behind them, they looked sadly back at their home, where their son was born, then stepped out into the dark night and to the unknown that lay ahead.

Chapter Three:
The Escape From Rovno

The train station was hit and mostly in ruins. Pillars of smoke rose everywhere, filling the air with the heavy odor of the fumes. Yet the place was bustling and teeming with people seeking a way out of the city. Rumor had it that the Nazis had already covered on the first day of battle half the distance between the western border and Rovno.

Rafal pushed his way through the crowds, leading Merie and the baby to platform number 5, which was closely guarded by a chain of soldiers who prevented anyone from approaching the train. Rafal showed his papers to the officer, who then allowed Merie and the baby to get on the train. Rafal hugged Merie tightly and kissed her and Alec who was nestled on Merie's chest. "Hey, Rafal, you're coming with us?" shouted Major Alexiev, the officer guarding the car.

"No, I'll be taking the next train with the Colonel. I'm putting my wife Merie and our son Alec in your care. Please help her if she'll need anything."

"Please, you can board the train," said Alexiev, "we'll find you a seat." Merie quickly kissed Rafal goodbye and climbed into the car. "Don't worry, your wife and son are safe," Alexiev told Rafal who stood forlornly on the platform, watching as the train pulled out heading east. Just then, the Colonel called him to help load the Archives' boxes on the next train that was leaving in the early morning hours.

Merie took her knapsack off her shoulders and placed it between her knees as she sat down with Alec on a bench at the end of the car. The rain stopped and the skies were clear. From the train window, Merie was looking at the star-studded sky when Major Alexiev walked past her. "Why are you worried?" she asked.

"The clearer and brighter the skies are, the greater the chances that the Germans will start bombing every moving thing. I hope the train will quickly put a significant distance between us..."

Alec began to cry. Merie gently turned his head towards her bare breast and let him nurse. What's your problem, she thought. You're warm, you're bound to your mother's belly and you're eating. As the train slowed down Merie glanced out the window at the soldiers standing near the train tracks that had been bombed and were being replaced with new tracks. Then the train picked up speed again and its monotonous motion soon lulled Merie and Alec to sleep.

The screeching of brakes jolted her up. The platform was filled with Russian soldiers running about, some firing into the air, others running for cover. The blasting noise of bomber planes came suddenly and a few seconds later, the entire train shook.

Merie stood up, a bit shaky, then grabbed her knapsack and threw it over her shoulder. Alec screamed and at that moment Major Alexiev came running past her and yelled, "Jump from the train and run to the forest. Wait an hour and if we manage to get the train running again, the train whistle will blow twice. Then you'll know you can come back and continue with us. If not, just keep on going east, for about thirty-five miles, in the same direction as the train. Hope to see you later," he said.

The train was moving very slowly. Merie stepped onto the lower step and grabbing the iron handle, she looked at to the damaged locomotive, and then jumped down off the train. The ground was covered with sharp stone fragments and her painful landing caused her to struggle to breathe. She rolled on her side while protecting Alec with both hands. Gunshots were heard everywhere. Soldiers of the Fifth Red Banner Army were mobilizing towards the battle. German planes kept circling in the air above, while she ran to the first line of forest trees about a hundred yards away from the train. When she felt she was safe amongst the trees, she stopped and looked at the train that sat like a huge animal's carcass on the tracks. Two German fighter planes with huge swastikas kept circling above and then dived toward the train dropping bombs on the train cars, which exploded with a thunderous sound into orange and yellow smoke columns. Two other planes attacked the remaining cars and the entire train went up in flames, killing anyone who hadn't yet managed to escape and destroying the entire cargo of the Russian Archives.

Alec, terrified, screamed. Merie sat down at the forest's edge, opened her shirt, and let Alec nurse, which calmed them both.

She recalled Alexiev telling her she must walk thirty-five miles eastward. She dropped the knapsack off her shoulder to discover that, a bag of diapers that was tied to the knapsack had fallen out when she jumped from the train and rolled on the ground. There was but one diaper left, and with that, she would have to make do. Half the money they had saved in the past year-and-a-half was rolled up in a tight wad and hidden in her bra. Rafal had the other half.

Merie knew that the treacherous forest lay at the lower southern border of the Pripyat Marshes, so she kept to the edge of the forest and was better protected from the German planes.

She wasn't alone on her foot journey to Kiev. After the bombed train's dead and wounded were vacated, the remaining soldiers and officers organized themselves into a group and

Merie joined them. She hurt all over from her jump off the train, and her coat was ripped.

Russian soldiers were marching along the train tracks toward the west. "That's the Fifth Red Banner Army on its way to position itself against the Germans," one officer told her. "It's the best equipped of all the Armies!"

After an hour of walking, Merie began to feel the heavy weight of the knapsack and the heavy coat, which grew even more superfluous as the day turned warmer, and Alec's weight clinging to her chest. Pain shot through her right foot, her ribs and right shoulder. She stopped, removed the knapsack and sat down to rest under a tree along the path. One of the soldiers sat down next to her and said, "I see you're having a hard time."

She looked at him. He seemed like a good fellow who was anxious to help. "What's your name?" she asked.

"I'm Private Arcadi Tiomkin, at your service, Ma'am," he saluted.

"If you could help me carry the knapsack, that would be great," Merie said.

"Gladly. I have no problem carrying your knapsack on top of mine."

Merie handed him her knapsack, opened her coat to help cool her body and they resumed walking. It was easier now and they managed to picked up their pace.

"Are you familiar with this area, Arcadi?" she asked.

"Yes, we're about thirty miles from Kiev. If we continue along the railway tracks, we'll reach the train bridge that crosses the Dnieper River. I don't know if it's passable, but there's a boat ferry that crosses every hour. If we continue walking near the trees, we'll be able to cover another fifteen miles by nightfall. I hope we come across some houses or barns where we can stay the night."

A whistle was heard from the east. A Russian locomotive was pushing a large crane heading west towards the burnt train.

"I'm not returning to the train, I'm going to continue to Kiev," Merie said.

"I'll accompany you," Arcadi said.

The sun began to set in the west. They had walked over eighteen miles and Merie was exhausted. Her right side was hurting and Alec was restless. She looked around her, hoping to spot a shelter for the night. Suddenly, she saw a wooden cabin that apparently served the forest rangers. Arcadi, Merie and some of the other soldiers headed towards it.

"At least we'll have a roof over our heads tonight," Merie said.

"But sadly we won't be able to light a fire and warm up," Arcadi answered. "There are very strict blackout regulations."

Everyone found themselves a corner, opened their knapsacks and took out some food. Merie took out the bread and the salami. She tore off a piece of bread and some salami and ate hungrily. It was her first morsel of food since the night before. Alec began to cry. She picked him up and carried him outside, several feet into the woods where she nursed him while rocking him, humming a lullaby her mother used to sing to her as a child. She dipped a rag into a puddle of water and washed the child and he smiled at her. "Thank you, sweetheart, that you're helping me." She kissed him, and then lay down on her coat spread out on the ground, held him close to her heart as they both fell asleep, an infant in his mother's arms.

Chapter Four: Kiev

The forest was rich in pine trees, as well as elm, oak and linden trees, nettle and blueberry bushes. Dappled light penetrated the leaves of and the sun's rays frolicked on the dewdrops. Merie finished taking care of Alec, tied the sheet wrap over her left shoulder, placed Alec in it and set off for Kiev. Suddenly hooves were heard, coming closer and a horse-drawn buggy appeared with a family of farmers riding in it. Arcadi raised his hand signaling them to stop. "Comrade, are you heading for Kiev?" he asked the buggy driver. "I have here a woman with an infant and they must reach Kiev quickly."

"Don't you see the buggy is full?"

"Yes, I see that. But there's someone waiting for the woman at the ferry boat, so can you please huddle in a little more and make room for her, or maybe one of you can get off." The buggy passengers crowded together. "She must reach the ferry boat as soon as possible," Arcadi added and the buggy driver nodded.

Merie took her knapsack from Arcadi, stood on her toes, and kissed him on his cheek.

"Thank you. I'll never forget you and how you helped me," she said.

She climbed into the buggy, which took off. The road running alongside the train tracks merged with the main road to Kiev, which was now packed with refugees making their way to the city. Some were pushing wagons, others placed all their belongings in baby carriages or on bikes. Every hour or so, German fighter planes swooped down on them and let loose bursts of machine gun fire unto the mob of refugees. Each time the planes approached, the buggy driver stopped and everyone jumped down seeking shelter from the gunfire. Merie always searched for a ditch, a tree, or a structure, and would lie down on the ground covering Alec with her body. After each such attack, dozens of dead bodies and the bleeding wounded were strewn along the road and in the fields. Merie shielded Alec's face protectively shying away from the gruesome carnage.

As they approached Kiev, the road grew more crowded with refugees and the buggy had a hard time moving forward through the crowds. Reaching the Dnieper River, Merie picked up her knapsack, thanked the buggy driver, got off and headed for the roadblock at the entrance to the ferry. Soldiers prevented the refugees from boarding it. "I was on the train that was bombed yesterday morning," Merie said and was immediately directed to the table positioned behind the soldiers, where two NKVD officers were sitting. Merie showed them her passport and again repeated her words, then added, "Major Alexiev, the train commander, told me to reach the Army headquarters."

One of the officers examined the passport. "Major Alexiev was killed during the bombing," he said and looked at Merie. "Since when does the Fifth Red Banner Army transport women with infants?"

"My husband is the consultant to the Army's Archives," she answered angrily, "and so they saw to it to evacuate us from Rovno with the archives." The officer returned her passport and said, "See here, lady, you're lucky. That group of soldiers over there, they've been arrested because they deserted their units. This evening they will all be executed. Better keep your voice low." Merie turned and walked towards the ferryboat that was tied to the dock of the west bank. But then she turned around and walked back to the officers' table. "One more thing," she said.

"There was a soldier on the train by the name of Arcadi Tiomkin, he was Alexiev's assistant. He was instructed to accompany me to Kiev. He should be reaching the roadblock, so please let him through – he has to report to the Army headquarters."

The soldier looked at her, wrote something down and nodded. "Continue on," he said.

Merie got on the crowded ferry. 'If I've helped increase Arcadi's chances of passing the roadblock,' Merie thought to herself, 'that will be his reward for helping me.' She leaned on the railing as the ferry pulled away from the riverbank and gazed at the water streaming beneath her. As the ferry reached the east bank she joined the crowd of refugees rushing to the main tram station. She searched for platform No.2, the electric tram to the Fifth Army headquarters. Most of the ferry passengers headed there too. When she got on the tram, a few soldiers gave her their seat so she took a load off and relaxed.

Merie had never been to Kiev so she looked out at the city curiously with its streets and buildings, which reminded her of Warsaw. The roads were jam-packed with cars and trams, and the sidewalks were bustling with people who seemed unaware that there was a war going on.

When the tram stopped near the Fifth Army headquarters, Merie got off, heading straight to the entrance gate where several soldiers stood, inspecting people's papers. She was sent to the officer in charge and explained that she was looking for her husband who was supposed to have arrived with the Colonel, the Archives commander. "Wait here, I'll see if I can find the Colonel." He dialed the Archives. "They said he stepped out to a meeting, he should be back any minute," he told her.

Exhausted Merie sat down on a nearby chair and her eyes dropped with fatigue. That was how Rafal found her an hour later, shocked to find his wife and son sleeping at the HQ entrance. He got down on his knees and burst in tears.

"Why are you crying?" Merie asked.

"I was sure you and Alec were killed..."

"Well, I and your little boy are fine and well, so don't cry," she kissed him. "All I need now is some rest. Let's find a hotel where I can take a shower, bandage my wounds and take care of Alec."

"Come," Rafal said taking his leave from the Colonel. "There's a small hotel across the street."

He helped Merie to get and took Alec from her. They crossed the road and entered the hotel where he got a room on the second floor. Alec dropped off immediately on the big bed and Merie quickly boiled water to bathe him and wash both their clothes. Rafal embraced her saying, "They said that everyone was killed. I was so frightened," he whispered in her ear and led her to the bed.

"Me too, I also wasn't sure I'd ever see you again," Merie said turning to him.

She lay down on the bed with tears rolling down her face. Rafal lay down beside her, careful of his infant son sleeping between them.

"I want us to leave, go away, as far away as possible, to Tashkent," she said. "You know we have to keep moving."

"The Army commander told us that as of now he's putting the archives on hold. The Colonel is waiting for a combat brigade so he's released me from service. We're free to go wherever we want. Tomorrow, before we leave, I'll stop by the Archives and get military travel passes for us. Now let's go to sleep, we've got a long way ahead of us."

The following morning, Rafal picked up the military travel passes, which granted them priority in boarding the train and getting seats. The Kiev train station was thronged with people, many trying to get on the train heading east. Rafal showed their travel passes to the officer in charge asking him to help them get on the eastbound train. The officer looked at the mob of people pushing their way on the platforms, then glanced at Merie and the baby, and said, "I'm afraid you won't be able to get on this train. Try again this evening. Maybe I'll be able to help you then."

They left the train station crossed the spacious square, and returned to the hotel. Rafal returned to the Army Headquarters to find any further help and returned in the evening ready to leave. "There's a train leaving for Poltava," he said. "It's halfway to Kharkov where there's a huge hub of trains."

"Rafal, I've got some cans of condensed milk in my knapsack that I bought in Rovno. You'll have to buy water and some food, I need to nurse Alec, and most importantly, don't take your eyes off my knapsack for one second."

It was dark when they left. The blackout rendered the streets and the houses covered with thick curtains and blankets, even darker. Merie and Rafal found their way across the square to the train station, which stood out against the sky. As earlier, the station was swarming with people trying to board every train that entered the station. Rafal was lost in the crowd and the only thing he could see was his head retreating from her. She felt she suffocated and crushed by the masses of people, fearing for Alec's safety.

Suddenly she felt the pressure receding. A squad of soldiers advanced toward her forming a chain that pushed back the crowds. Rafal walked towards her escorted by an officer.

"This is a military train that's heading for Poltava. The Colonel is letting us board."

The car they entered was packed with families of army officers and senior party officials. Rafal managed to find them seats and Merie sat down and began nursing Alec, with Rafal next to her covering her breast.

"This is no time to be ashamed," she said. "We have an infant who has to feed and I'll nurse him anywhere and everywhere." After the baby stopped nursing, she handed him over to her husband and fell asleep. Rafal remained awake, embracing his infant son as the train rushed on through the darkness, leaving the war behind.

Chapter Five: Air Strike

At sunrise, the speeding train slowed down and shook all over as it came to a full stop. Soldiers ran alongside checking the train's wheels and after a half an hour stop it slowly rumbled into the train station at the town of Velikiye, to where it was sidetracked and stopped.

It turned out that two of the locomotive's wheels had cracked and where in danger of buckling. The passengers had to wait for a replacement locomotive to arrive from Kharkov so the journey could continue.

"We might have to wait a few days until a new locomotive arrives. All the trains are conscripted to dismantle high-priority factories and are being sent east," Rafal said.

Merie nursed Alec and changed his diaper, using the last one she had left, after losing the package of diapers during her flee from the burning train. She asked Rafal to go and try to find diapers, bread and dried salami for their ongoing journey.

Just then the hum of planes was heard coming from the west with the whistling sound, familiar from Warsaw, and the screeching of the Stuka planes diving and dropping bombs. Merie rushed to the car door as the Stuka planes circled over the town's houses dropping their bombs. All around them buildings were going up in flames and collapsing. She rushed out of the train towards a small cement structure nearby while bombs were falling on the train station. The ground shook.

After half an hour, which seemed like an eternity, the planes receded and silence prevailed. Merie stepped out of her shelter to look at the station's buildings which were burning and black smoke covered the blue skies. Miraculously, the train itself wasn't damaged. As people began to come out of their hiding places, the screams of the wounded were heard from the train station. Within minutes, firefighters arrived along with ambulances and medical teams who began treating the wounded.

Merie returned to the train car that was filling up with soldiers. As time passed and Rafal did not return, she became worried. Perhaps he got hurt from the bombing. She stepped off the train and began pacing back and forth on the platform. Just then the replacement locomotive pulled in, and Merie realized that the train would be pulling out soon. But Rafal was nowhere in sight.

She boarded the train, breathing heavily, and walked to the bench that had become their home. Rafal was sitting there, smiling.

"I was so worried about you!" She cried.

He told her in a hushed voice, "In town, I met one of General Kirponos's senior officers and he told me that Stalin increased the number of divisions sent to the front, but forbade Kirponos to retreat from Kiev. A German tank unit unexpectedly turned southward, conquered Gomel and is about to hook up with the German forces coming up from the south. If they succeed, they will surround the Fifth Army, including Kiev, which will mean the total collapse of the Soviet defense in central Ukraine."

"What are you saying?" Merie asked.

"I'm saying that the sooner this train starts out again, the better it will be for us and our son. But, remember, you're not to mention a word I just told you to anyone. As far as you know, the Soviet army is courageously halting the fascist Germans. Under these circumstances we won't be able to remain in Kharkov either."

"So where will we go?"

"From Kharkov, as far as we can get to the other side of the Volga River. I say we head southeast," Rafal answered.

"In other words, Tashkent," Merie said. "Everyone says it's the 'breadbasket' city, the most important commodity in the war."

"Let's not exaggerate," Rafal replied, "no need to escape to the end of the world."

The train began moving eastward, leaving behind Velikiye's smoking station. With every mile, the train covered eastward, Merie felt more relieved.

Chapter Six:
From Kharkov To Stalingrad

It was dark when the train finally pulled into Kharkov. . The station was swarming with people looking for a way to get to the east. "I'm afraid it will be more difficult here for us," Rafal said. "I don't have any connections with the military here."

Disembarking, Merie found a quieter corner in the station and sat down on the floor, hugging Alec close to her. As her eyes dropped of exhaustion, she was suddenly shaken awake by a hand on her shoulder. "Merie!" Rafal cried, "Come quickly! There's a train which we must get on." He helped her up and began running, clearing a path for her through the crowds. They reached the far end of Platform No.3, as Rafal pushed open the door of the last car, which was packed with people. The train started pulling away from the station as Merie stood at the car's very edge near the door, while Rafal held on, balancing himself on the outside steps. He managed to hang on to the metal sidebar and survived an hour of traveling by gripping the handle tightly. Merie was squashed between the mass of people protecting Alec as best she could. Gradually, the pressure of the crowd let up and Rafal managed to climb into the car. Only then did she ask, "Where are we going?"

"Stalingrad," Rafal answered.

Merie frowned. "We were supposed to head east towards the Volga. Stalingrad's in the south and the war's going on there too, the Germans reached Crimea already, haven't they?"

"Yes," answered Rafal. "And from there it will be easier for us to get on an eastbound train and then we'll decide if we continue to Tashkent or stay in Saratov."

"How long's the ride?" Merie asked.

"I figure it'll take a few days. I'm going to look for a better place for you and the baby. I'll be back in an hour." Indeed, an hour later he returned. "Follow me," he said, "I found a spot for you and Alec on a bench in the third car. I'll stand next to you, so we can change places on the bench every few hours. Give me the knapsack and hold Alec."

Merie handed her knapsack to Rafal and they began making their way through the dense masses. When they reached the third car, Rafal indicated a bench on which sat a Russian peasant woman. "Mrs. Yosibov," Rafal said, "this is my wife Merie and our son Alec." Mrs. Yosibov glanced at Merie and made room for her on the bench next to her. Merie quickly sat down and thanked her.

The train ride to Stalingrad took seven days and every few hours the train was sidetracked to allow trains coming from the opposite direction. Occasionally, the train would stop in a town along the tracks to let the passengers get off and stretch their legs. Rafal would rush into the town, buy food and fill bottles with water. Once he even managed to buy a white sheet. Merie was thrilled to see it. She ripped it into twelve squares and used them as diapers.

The days started merging as the journey continued, as the small family got more and more tired and depleted.

Finally, after ten days of exhausted traveling since leaving Kiev, the train pulled into the resplendent train station of Stalingrad. Leaving the station, they saw the famous statue of boys and girls dancing in a circle, in the central square. It was one of the city's famous trademarks.

"Let's find a hotel," Merie said. "I want to get cleaned up and bathe Alec and sleep."

Rafal looked around him. "Maybe we'll find a small room here on the square," he said.

They tried a hotel at the other end, but there were no vacancies available. Nor were there any rooms available in the other two hotels they checked. Finally, on a small side street, they found a small hotel that had one room left which they took. After weeks of traveling and meandering between train stations, Merie finally could enjoy a warm shower and bathe Alex, wash their clothes, and sleep on a proper bed with sheets. She knew, however, that their stay there was brief, being close to the war front. That night Alec let her sleep. He too was exhausted and woke up as late as early morning to eat.

Rafal went out to scout the city and returned with a wide grin on his face. "What are you so happy about?" Merie asked.

"Let me tell you, of all the cities we've been to, this one is the most modern. You won't believe how wide the Volga River is, it's more than two thousand feet of flowing water. There are boats floating on it, and huge factories along its banks. I'm certain that the two of us, a nurse and an archive expert, will be able to do well here. How about it? Shall we make this our home?"

Merie thought for a few moments, searching for the right words, and then said in a quiet yet determined voice, "Rafal, you can stay here if you wish. Alec and I are continuing eastward. You were lucky that you didn't run into any Germans in Warsaw, so there are some things you'll never understand."

"Where do you want to run to, the end of the world? What will be far enough for you, Palestine?"

"Eretz Yisrael is a good option," Merie answered. "It's better than the war."

"Palestine is not an alternative to anything!" Rafal yelled. "The Germans and Italians are beating the British in the desert, and are threatening Palestine. You don't understand, in today's world no place is safe!"

"When we were still in Rovno, I told you that we're heading for Tashkent. I'm going there with or without you. As I see it, whether it's three hundred miles or six hundred miles from the front, it's never far enough."

"And I thought that after weeks of running from place to place on crowded trains, with a baby in your arms and surviving two air strikes, you'd be glad to finally settle down," Rafal said. "The Germans can also reach Tashkent."

"You're right," Merie said. "But practically speaking, until the Germans reach Tashkent we'll have time to think where to escape to."

"And what will we do there?" He said.

"I heard that the Russians are organizing and training army divisions in Tashkent. Many refugees are signing up, and I'm sure we'll be able to find work there and a place to live. Near the Volga would have been nicer, but Tashkent is safer."

"Okay, I understand. I agree. Let's rest here for a few days and I'll check out the train schedules to Tashkent and buy tickets. I'm exhausted."

Chapter Seven:
From Stalingrad To Tashkent

"**W**e've got a problem," Rafal said when he returned to their hotel room the following day. "We can't buy tickets to Tashkent because we don't have visas. Our papers are valid only inside the Russian zone, and the police refused to issue visas because our documents define us as refugees from the western zone, Poland that's under German control. So I bought us tickets to Saratov. Most Russians cannot enter Saratov. I told them we're going there to meet with the leaders of the Polish government-in-exile now being formed. They phoned Saratov to check and it turns out they know who I am. Of course they would, these are my friends from the Communist cell at Warsaw University. Do you remember Henryk Jabłoński?"

"Yes, he went to high school with you and then to Warsaw University together, and continued on to your Ph.D. So we're not just moving on, we're going to meet and consult with them." Rafal's face lit up with a broad smile.

"So what are you actually saying?" Merie asked.

"I suggest we get to the train station early tomorrow morning. There's a train leaving at eight o'clock. Thanks to my well-connected friends, we'll be able to get visas to the east, God willing."

"Since when do you use the words 'God willing'?" Merie asked, surprised. She didn't know whether to laugh or cry.

"Since I studied in the Heder in Tomaszow Mazowiecki," Rafal answered, laughing. "My parents, bless their memory, saw to it that I wouldn't forget my true origins."

"So be it," Merie said, hugging Alec. "We'll go to Saratov, meet Jabłoński and your Communist friends, have coffee with them, create and destroy nations, everything's fine. But remember one thing, we're on our way to Tashkent, nowhere else."

Rafal kissed her Merie. "No need for concern," he said and bent over Alec, tickling his belly. "We've got a trip of about forty-five miles ahead of us and we'd best remain patient and level-headed. Your 'breadbasket city' isn't going to allocate living quarters to us if we don't have work, and we won't get food coupons either, and without food coupons, we'll starve to death. So we really need my friends' help over there."

There weren't many people at the train station early the next morning. The train pulled out and slowly increased speed, and from the car window, they could watch Volga River flowing slowly as if there was no war in the world. Merie gazed at her husband who was holding their son, and said a silent prayer.

As the train pulled into Saratov station and Merie and Rafal stepped down, they were surprised to see Henrik Jabłoński waiting for them. They embraced him warmly. "How did you know we're arriving?" Rafal asked.

"I was in touch with a friend who works with the Rails Authority and he kept me posted on your progress, or rather the many unexpected stops that caused the delay."

"Luckily, the Rails Authority saw to it that we'd stop in train stations where they cooked soup for us and gave us each a slice of bread," Rafal said. "Henrik, tell me, could our friend in the Government Companies Authority help us get visas to Tashkent?"

Jabłoński looked at Rafal, surprised. "Why Tashkent? What's wrong with staying here? It's a great city. All our university friends are here, we can arrange a good job for you and living accommodations."

Rafal glanced at Merie and said, "There's no point getting into that now."

"What's wrong with Saratov?" Henrik asked.

"It's too close to the front," Merie said.

"Too close?" he repeated her words. "We're about six hundred miles from the front!"

"The Germans have already proven they can cover such a distance in ten days," Merie replied. "Henrik, Rafal and I discussed this at length. If it were up to him, we'd still be in Kiev or in Poltava, and the Germans have conquered both places for quite a while."

"Okay," Henrik said, "I suggest we first go to your hotel, settle in and then Rafal can come with me to the Polish Delegation House and meet his friends from the university. As to the visa, give me your passports, if you don't mind, and don't worry. If you insist on continuing to Tashkent, we'll arrange visas for you and a comfortable seat on the train. It's a pretty crazy trip, nearly two thousand miles. It'll take you several weeks, not days."

The taxi stopped in front of a three-story building, and Jabłoński asked the cab driver to wait. They got to their room through a small lobby and Jabłoński looked pleased with his friends' reaction to their room, which had a private bathroom. "The government-in-exile in Saratov will pay for your stay here. So settle in, shower and rest. I'll return this afternoon to pick up Rafal. Everyone's dying to meet you already."

As evening fell, Merie and Rafal relaxed on the balcony facing a garden filled with fruit trees. Rafal told her all about his visit to the headquarters of the Polish government-in-exile. "My friends from Warsaw and from the university's Communist cell and were anxious to hear all about our escape from the Germans, and I'm delighted to say, I was offered a position here with the establishment committee. What do say?"

Merie looked at her excited husband and said, "Rafal, how many times do I have to tell you?"

"Okay, don't get excited or angry," Rafal said. "I tried my luck. Day after tomorrow, we'll get our tickets and passports with permits to travel east."

The train heading towards Uzbekistan was full of officers and their families, on their way to army training units in the east. Since their role in the war effort was vital, the train made good and managed to get there in just under two weeks. And just like the train from Stalingrad to Saratov, this train too stopped twice a day at stations where huge vats of soup were waiting to provide them with nourishment. During the day, Merie and Rafal shared one bench. At night, Rafal slept on the luggage shelf above them while she slept with Alec on the bench.

During the late morning hours of a warm and sunny day, the train reached Tashkent. The station was full of local merchants trying to sell their wares. Merie and Rafal knew no one in Tashkent. Their entire world possessions were packed in their two knapsacks. Alec, who had grown up during the long and exhausting voyage, stared inquisitively at the new city. Suddenly, Merie heard a high clear voice singing a Hebrew song she knew from her years in Pinsk with the Hashomer Hatzair movement.

"Why are you crying?" Rafal asked.

"That's the song by Rachel the poetess, which we used to sing at the Hashomer nest. We're not alone..."

Merie drew closer to the young girl singer who was wearing worn but clean clothes. Her thick black braid fell down her back and her brown eyes studied Merie curiously. When she finished singing, she smiled and asked in Hebrew, "Were You with the Hashomer youth movement?"

Merie nodded, then asked, "And who are you?"

"My name's Lydia and I'm the 'sounding board.'"

"The sounding board?"

"I'm a live bulletin board that speaks as well as hears. I'm here every day, waiting for the trains bringing in the refugees and I sing the songs that were sung in the Movement. Every single person who was in Hashomer Hatzair stops here in front of me, and many have tears in their eyes, like you. I refer them to an apartment we rented in Tashkent, and that's how we gather together the Movement's members that are arriving from the west and from Siberia."

"Who's coordinating the activities at this apartment?" Merie asked.

"Etka, she's from Rovno," Lydia answered.

"Etka..." Merie repeated with a whisper, and another tear slid down her face.

Chapter Eight: Tashkent

The Movement's apartment was located on a small street off the main road and the train station. On their way to the meeting, Merie said, "If I hadn't insisted that we keep on moving and come here, we'd have already been under Nazi rule."

Rafal gave her an angry look. "No one has conquered Stalingrad yet."

Merie scoffed, "Yet. That's the key word."

"I see you've become an expert on war strategy," Rafal said as they climbed up the steps of an old building and Merie knocked on the door. Etka, her friend from Rovno, opened the door and stared at them.

"I don't believe it...is that you, Merie?" Etka cried, hugging her.

"Have I changed that much?" Merie chuckled.

"Merie! I was so worried you'd never make it out of Rovno. Remember when we met just a few days before the Russian invasion?"

Merie nodded. "Etka, this is my husband, Rafal, and Alec who you've met already."

Etka shook Rafal's hand, then placed a kiss on Alec's cheek and folded him in her arms. Alec looked at her with his deep brown eyes, then stretched out his arms to his mother.

"No better place than Mom," Etka said and handed Alec back to Merie.

"Come in, there is tea and a slice of bread. Sorry, but we don't have much more than that."

"We still have some food left from our journey," Merie said. "Let's organize a joint meal and you'll tell us how to get settled." She placed the food they had on a woolen blanket spread out on the floor, and they all sat down. "I'm not used to eating without the train's motion," Merie laughed. "Okay, tell us what's going on."

"This apartment is the Movement's headquarters in Uzbekistan," Etka said and took a bite from her bread dipping it in the soup. "Most of our members are sent here by the 'sounding board.' The city is overrun with refugees, so we divided them into kibbutzim and collectives. These groups are dispersed all along the rail lines from Tashkent to the peripheral towns, and they are the ones that give us strength. For example, Movement members from Rovno have formed a collective called *Baminhara* [in the tunnel] in a city south of Tashkent. The heads of the Asia movement are Mordechai Rosman and Motak Rotman. They arrived here with a group from Vilna.

Merie, Tashkent is a honey trap."

"I figured as much," Rafal said.

"There isn't enough food and accommodations for everyone," Etka explained, "so we're sending our people to small towns and villages where things are easier. It's very hard to manage on your own."

"We'll stay here," Merie said.

"First of all, you have to find employment. That's the only way you'll be able to rent a room, a space. I'm using those terms because apartments aren't available. The only apartments for rent that you'll find are just huts with flattened earth as floors. Without a job and a place to live, you won't get a booklet of food stamps, and without that, you'll starve."

Rafal stretched his back. "In that case, I'd better go talk to Army Headquarters. Can Merie and Alec stay here and wait till I return?"

"Certainly," Etka replied. "I suggest you start with the Russian Forces Headquarters, right across from the train station."

"Thanks, Etka," Rafal said and kissed Merie. "I didn't expect to find such an organized, effective network."

Etka and Merie were left alone.

Etka began preparing lunch. "You never know who's going to show up unexpectedly," she said. "The Movement members know they can always find a bowl of soup and a slice of bread here, as well as a postal address, especially for corresponding with the Movement in Palestine. That's why we're maintaining this apartment.

What are your plans?" she asked.

"I'm pretty sure I'll be able to find work in one of the hospitals. But what will I do with Alec?"

Etka didn't answer, b trying to think. Suddenly, she perked up. "Merie, listen, I've got a much better idea for you. The hospitals aren't going anywhere. I suggest you first go to the Jewish Orphanage. That's where we send children who arrive here without their parents. They have a nursery school there, and maybe you'll be able to work there and keep Alec with you."

"Sounds like a good idea," Merie said, helping Etka prepare the vegetables for the soup. Etka smiled happily and said, "Lydia is on her way so we'll leave Alec with her and I'll take you to the orphanage."

Just then, Alec woke up and Merie tended to him.

Just then, Lydia walked in and gave Etka a quick kiss on her cheek. "I see you found the right apartment," she said to Merie, "and I understand there's soup..."

"Vegetable soup and a slice of bread."

Merie looked at her fondly. "I was so anxious about coming to Tashkent," she said to Lydia. "But the moment I heard you singing, I knew I wasn't alone. That's the last thing I would have expected to find in an Uzbekistan train station, soft, clear singing in Hebrew..."

"Thanks, Merie, that's our aim. Etka, you're a magician, how do you manage to turn so few ingredients into such a delicious soup?" Lydia said as she took a taste.

They left Alec in her care and headed toward the Jewish Orphanage. They walked down the narrow street up to the train station's square, where they boarded a No.5 tram. Though the city was big, it seemed dusty and old. "Since the war broke out, mobs of refugees from Poland and Siberia have swarmed the city, hoping to find food and shelter," Etka said. "But they didn't and the situation isn't easy. If you find work, you'll be able to stay here. If not, you'll have to continue on to the peripheral towns." Merie listened to Etka as she continued gazing out the tram window. She noticed piles of bodies wrapped in rags on the street corners. "Those people died during the night," Etka whispered. "Some starved to death, others died from typhus or cholera. Every day at noon, the city wagons go through the streets and collect the bodies for burial in mass graves outside the city, just like in the Middle Ages in Europe."

The tram continued and the further it got from the train station, the greater the number of dead bodies was.

The two young women walked along a narrow road, which ended in a compound surrounded by a brick wall. Etka opened the gate. "Welcome to the Jewish Orphanage in Tashkent," she said in a formal tone.

In the center of the compound stood the administration building which also housed the dining room and classrooms. Across from it, stood about twenty mud huts, which housed the children and in between lay a wide playground and a bathroom structure.

Etka turned to the director's office, Ella Davidovich, and knocked lightly on the door.

"Hi Ella," she said. "I'd like you to meet Merie who just arrived in Tashkent with her husband and baby."

Ella looked up from the documents she was studying. She was a tall woman, very thin, with an elongated face and black-rimmed eyeglasses rested on her nose. She had on a wide, grey dress that was too big for her. Her hair was gathered in a bun on her neck.

"What brings you here?" she asked.

"Merie is a registered nurse who specializes in treating children. I know you need a nurse ever since the previous one left. I thought it would serve all parties well if Merie could work here, instead of looking for a job at a hospital."

Ella looked interested and after asking Merie about her previous employment, she said, "With your experience and your special training, it will be our pleasure to accept you here. But, sadly, I can't pay you. We get our funds from the government and the Jewish community and they are earmarked for purchasing food and medication for the children and staff. You can stay in one of the buildings in the compound. We have a professional caretaker for the infants, so that will allow you to be free to treat the children and, believe me, you'll have your hands full."

Merie glanced at Etka, who nodded in agreement, as if to say, 'Grab the offer, it's the best you'll get.'

"I'll be glad to accept," Merie said. "When can I begin?"

For the first time since they met, Ella smiled. She shook Merie's hand and said, "Come, let me show you around and most importantly, I'll introduce you to the children. Our biggest problem right now is the epidemics."

As the three women entered the classroom the children were sitting along the walls and on benches. They had on clothes that were too big for them, but they were all clean. They gazed at the women with sad eyes. Ella smiled and said, "Children, this is Merie and she is the nurse who will take care of you as of tomorrow."

On the way back to the Movement's apartment, Merie recalled the long, exhausting journey she had been through from the day she had left Rovno with the outbreak of war, and her eyes filled with tears. For the first time in a very long time, she felt solid ground under her.

Chapter Nine:
The Orphanage

When they returned to the Movement apartment, Merie hugged Rafal all excited and told him about the living-quarters and the job at the city's Jewish orphanage.

"Well, unfortunately, I don't have good news," Rafal said. "I was told that the military archives have been merged with the national archives. I asked for an interview with the director, but he won't be in this week."

"Rafal, what matters most is that we're safe. Do you have any idea of the work conditions and the salary you might get?"

"I spoke with the deputy director, Galina Yosifoba. I told her that I served as deputy director of the archives in the Rovno area and was also in charge of the archives of the Fifth Red Banner Army. She thinks the jobs I held will help me get the position. She said that if I were accepted, my salary would be the same as that of Uzbekistani civil workers, which means not high, and as for accommodations, they cannot help with that at all. But, the workers get food coupon booklets for themselves and their families. We'll just have to wait until the archives director returns. Turns out that he's the brother of the Secretary of the Uzbekistan Communist Party, and Galina promised to help me get an appointment."

"That's great," Merie said. "At least we've got a room at the orphanage, and we'll also get our meals there and Alec will be in the infants' nursery."

"If I get the job at the archives, we'll be able to get a decent apartment, but meanwhile the current solution works well."

Rafal shouldered their knapsacks, and Merie lifted Alec, complaining how heavy he's gotten. She hugged Etka goodbye, as she and Rafal left to take the tram to the orphanage.

From the windows of the tram, they looked out at the Uzbekistani people dressed in their traditional garb and colorful hats, with their slightly oriental eyes and olive-dark skin. The streets were filled with refugees in rags and little children stood on the corners with their hands out begging for a pittance. Smoke rose everywhere, from the burning piles of rubbish in an attempt to prevent the spread of epidemics. Merie looked away as she spotted a pile of long white body bags with the previous night's corpses.

As they went in, they saw the central yard of the orphanage bustling with children playing. They all stopped as they spotted the strangers and they quickly gathered around Merie and Rafal. Ella walked up to them calling out: "Recess over! Back to class, everybody!" and the children scurried to their classrooms.

"Welcome!" Ella kissed Merie on the cheek and shook Rafal's hand. He kissed the back of her hand, to which Ella responded, "Polish manners. How refreshing." She stroked Alec's cheek, saying, "What this child has been through these past months... at least you got away from the war front. Come, I'll show you your room." They followed her as she opened the door. "it's not a palace," she said, "but believe me, this is as good as it gets. We'll bring you a pitcher of water and a bowl to wash up in the morning, and a woolen blankets you can spread out on the floor and cover yourselves. You'll also be given an oil lamp to light up the room, and that's it, you're all set."

It was small, the walls built of mud bricks with only one door. The roof was made of twigs covered with a thick layer of straw and the floor was tightly pressed earth. A wardrobe with a missing leg stood in a corner. Rafal looked at Merie who glanced back at him and shrugged her shoulders. "Where can we wash up?" she asked.

"There's a bath house not far," Ella said. "We shower the children there once a week and the staff goes there in the evenings. The meals are served in the dining hall, which is also our meeting hall and party venue. I suggest you settle in and come to the dining hall in half an hour. You'll meet the staff and the children, and the director of the infants' nursery will look after your son."

Merie and Rafal looked around at the room and at each other again.

"I realize we won't find anything better than this in town. Let's hope you get the job with the national archives and then we'll start buying some furniture."

She placed Alec down on the cold floor and spread out the blanket that would serve as their bed and the second one on top of it. Alec began crawling and sat up in the center of the blanket. Rafal went out in search of a stone which he then placed under the wardrobe to stabilize it and Merie put their knapsacks away in it. Then they walked over to the central dining hall.

The room was large lined with long tables at which sixty children of different ages were sitting. A dozen staff members were sitting at another table. Ella invited them to sit next to her, then picked up a knife and tapped on a metal teapot. The room fell quiet.

"I would like to introduce you to Merie and Rafal Gerber and their infant son, Alec," she said. "They've come to us after a very long and difficult journey from Rovno in western Ukraine. Merie is a registered nurse who graduated from the Nursing School in Warsaw, and will now be the nurse here at our institute. As you all know, many people succumbed to typhus and cholera in Tashkent, so for that purpose, we have an isolation room, as well as medications for treating cholera and we make sure to drink a lot. Merie will look after you." Ella nodded to Merie.

Merie stood up and looked at the pale faces of the children and the staff. "I'm glad to be here with you, after our long journey escaping from the Nazis," she said and her eyes filled with tears. "On the way here, I noticed the piles of rubbish everywhere and the bodies of the dead. This means that infectious diseases such as cholera and typhus are permanent residents of this city." Everyone nodded in agreement. "Here at this compound, in our crowded living conditions, an epidemic can break out any minute. Typhus, especially the typhoid variety, is far more dangerous. Most of those who catch it, unfortunately, die in great pain. But whoever survives the first ten days of the disease, will recover. If each and every one of us makes sure to wash their hands before every meal, we'll be able to prevent the outbreak of the epidemic. Let's start with that. Before I treat any child or adult, I will inspect the bathroom and the water sources," she added filled with determination and a sense of calling.

Chapter Ten:
Epidemic

Boiruch was the first to reach the infirmary. He threw up, couldn't hold any food down and had severe diarrhea. Merie hooked him to an IV with fluids and gave him a pill to bring down his fever. Several hours later, Boiruch was showing some improvement.

"Don't forget the potty if you get a diarrhea attack," Merie told him and pointed to the receptacle near his bed. She knew that Boiruch was the leader of a gang of orphan boys who often raided the market stalls and stole food items. The market venders had caught him a few times and beaten him, and he would then return to the orphanage with a large bruise on his face or an open wound in his forehead, but smiling.

"Don't tell Ella," he asked her.

"Tell me where your friends are."

"At the market, and... they didn't steal anything today...," Boiruch murmured as he sank into a deep sleep.

Merie washed her hands and left for Ella's office. She ran into Ada Greenberg who directed the adolescent children's department.

"I'm afraid the epidemic has reached us," Merie said. "Boiruch is suffering from fever, vomiting, diarrhea and headaches. I hope it's just food poisoning, but I suspect it's cholera. I'd like to check the others in his group. I'm sure that whatever Boiruch ate, they did too. I'll prepare the isolation room so that I can separate the healthy children from the sick. Also, please tell Zoya that I must leave Alec in her care until late tonight. Now I'm off, to find the gang."

"I'll tell her," Ada said and added, "Merie, there are Jewish children who were sent to the convents because there wasn't room for them here, but now the Catholics are wiping out any Polish presence in Tashkent, and I don't know what will become of them?"

"I didn't know that," Merie said. "I'll see what I can do. But now we have to focus on solving this epidemic."

Ella was in the middle of a meeting with the administrator, the cook and the treasurer when Merie barged into her office. "I'm sorry to disturb you," she said, "but Boiruch has clear symptoms of cholera. If any of the children have caught the disease, it will spread here like wildfire. This is an epidemic, and a very bad one. We'll need two isolation rooms, and infusion bottles for fluids, pills against vomiting and pain, and a great deal of luck."

"We were just talking about our lack of funds and have to cut back on our food supplies," Ella said.

"And there are restrictions on bread allotment, It's been reduced to fourteen ounces per day for adults and nine ounces per child," the treasurer added.

Merie spread out her arms. "If we don't get infusion bottles and medication, we'll have corpses. I'm on my way to take a feces specimen from Boiruch and check it at the Central Hospital labs, that's the only way we'll know where we stand."

The treasurer shook his head. "I don't know where we can get the money for infusion bottles and medication."

Merie gazed long and hard at Ella and the treasurer and asked, "What if we take out a loan for a month or two, will we be able to pay it back?"

"I believe within two or three months we'll be able to do that." Ella said.

"Okay," Merie said. "Can I have a container for the lab test?"

The treasurer pulled out a matchbox from his pocket, dumped its contents on the table and handed it to Merie. "That's all I have. Wrap it up in a newspaper, and good luck!"

On her way back to the infirmary, Merie saw the entire gang waiting for her, together with Ada. She stood them all in line and asked, "Does any one of you have headaches?" The boys looked at one another and nodded their heads 'No.' "Does anyone here have diarrhea?" The children laughed and again shook their heads 'No.' "Listen up," she said sharply. "This is no joke. Boiruch is very sick with a disease that you can die from. It's highly contagious, but if it's caught on time, there's a chance to live through it. I'm going to ask you once again. Is there anyone here who is not feeling?" The boys lowered their heads and shook 'No' for an answer. "Good. From this moment on, you will all be staying together in isolation in one room with no contact with anyone on this compound. You will be given food and drink, we'll bring you buckets filled with water. You will wash your hands before you eat, and before and after any hand contact with someone else. I'm going to the hospital now, so if anyone feels ill, go to Ada."

"Can we visit Boiruch?" Shloimele asked.

Merie's first instinct was to say no, but she then changed her mind. "Absolutely. In fact, you will take turns. Each time, one of you will be responsible for emptying his potty into the toilet. Then you have to thoroughly wash the potty with water and scrub your hands with soap and water. You'll do the same with the potties that will be put in your room."

The children looked at Merie with fear in their eyes. Merie knew that this was the only way she could make sure they would wash their hands. She took Ada's hand and pulled her away to the side. "If anyone starts feeling sick, put him in the isolation room near the infirmary," she said. "I hope I scared them enough..."

As Merie entered the infirmary, the potty standing near the bed gave off a sickening smell. She took a tiny specimen and placed it in the matchbox, then wrapped it in a newspaper and went out to the main street and got on the tram, with her handbag over her shoulder, holding her tiny package hoping its odor wouldn't chase away the passengers. The closer to the city center they got, the cleaner the streets appeared.

Merie got off the tram near the train station and headed for the Movement's apartment. Etka welcomed her with a warm embrace. There was a young man of about thirty years of age who was sitting at the table. He had a headful of thick, black hair, and looked tired.

"Say hello to Motak Rotman," Etka said. "He's head of the Hashomer Hatzair in Asia and he's here to meet with General Anders and the Polish Embassy. We're trying to bring together all the members of our and of other movements to join the Polish army and fight the Nazis, and then also reach Palestine."

Motak shook Merie's hand. "I've heard a lot about you and your work at the orphanage from Etka. Stay strong."

Merie smiled. "Like the oath of Hashomer Hatzair," she said. "As for oaths... this isn't a social call, it's an emergency. It seems one of the children at the orphanage has contacted cholera." Etka pulled back in fright. "I must buy medication to fight the epidemic if it breaks out, and the orphanage has no funds at all for this. Could you possibly lend me several hundred rubles so I can buy the medicines? Our treasurer says we could return it within two or three months, when the funds from the Joint come in."

Motak glanced at Etka. "Do we have any reserves?" he asked. Etka nodded.

"How much do you think we can lend without harming our operations?" He asked.

"I think about three hundred rubles," Etka replied.

"That's better than nothing," Merie said. "It's a lifesaver."

"Okay. I approve our lending three hundred rubles from our reserve funds to the Jewish orphanage for medicines. Merie will be responsible to see the loan is returned."

"Thank you," Merie said. "I guarantee it."

"I also have a favor to ask of you," Motak said. "My main activities are keeping contact between the kibbutz groups that settled along the railroad tracks. We call them 'tracks.' We ride the train at pre-specified times and the groups' representatives wait for us at the stations. We coordinate their activities and help them with any problems that come up. There are kibbutz groups along the tracks, between Tashkent and Samarkand, that have health problems. I would like you to join me on one of these trips and check them. Could you do that?"

"Besides being committed to the orphanage," Merie said, "are you aware that I have a one-year-old infant?"

Motak nodded. "Of course, we'll have to find a solution to that."

"I'll be glad to help. I'll have to get Ella's agreement and check with my husband Rafal. I'll give you my answer through Etka. How long is the trip to Samarkand?"

"Anywhere from three to six days," Motak said. "It depends on how long each stop lasts at the stations."

Merie sighed. "I'll need a bag of medical supplies and first-aid items," she said.

"Etka will buy whatever medications you need and prepare the bag."

Etka left the room and returned with a roll of bills. "Here's three hundred rubles," she said.

"Thank you," Merie kissed her on the cheek, then said to Motak, "I hear rumors that there are plans to remove the Jewish children from the Catholic convents and send them to Eretz Yisrael. When you meet General Anders, ask him about the Jewish orphanage."

"I will," Motak said.

Merie left the apartment on her way to the Central Hospital. Entering the main hall, she turned towards the lab's reception window in front of which a long line of people stood waiting. She asked a nurse who passed by for help and the nurse signaled her to follow her to the lab, where she took the package with the specimen from her.

"What's your name?" Merie asked.

"I'm Ludmila," the nurse said shaking her hand.

"Could I possibly get your help on another matter?" Merie asked. Ludmila nodded. "I need some infusion bottles in case the epidemic spreads. Could you let me have some from your supplies?"

"We're not allowed to take infusion bottles out of the hospital," Ludmila replied. "But if you don't have them, the children will end up here in the hospital," she smiled, so "I'll give you four bottles, but when you're through with them, you must return them."

"Of course I'll return them," Merie said.

She took the bottles, purchased the medicines at the pharmacy and rushed back to the orphanage.

"Shloimele and Yoel have diarrhea. We put them in the infirmary," Ella told her as she entered the compound.

"We isolated them. They're both in the room with Boiruch."

Merie told Ella what she brought back from the hospital and Ella was moved to tears. "I'll report to the treasurer and he'll see to it to return the money," she said. "Thank you for everything you're doing, there are so many orphaned children, and now this disease."

Merie hugged Ella and they walked over to the isolation room. Shloimele and Yoel were sitting on the potties and Boiruch was lying in bed with his eyes shut.

"You can let everyone know that the cholera epidemic has reached the orphanage," Merie said.

Chapter Eleven:
Matchboxes

A fter two weeks of fighting for the children's recovery, everyone was beginning to show signs of recuperation. The first was Boiruch, who was into everything and everywhere. He was sitting on his bed, having soup when Merie pulled up a chair in front of him and said, "Boiruch, I want to appoint you as the kingpin responsible for a very important part of the orphanage. I want you and your gang, once you're all well again, to be our 'Cleaning Police.'"

Boiruch looked at Merie with an amused look in his eyes. "Will we get police hats and uniforms?" He asked.

Merie smiled. "I'll see what we can do about that. But, you must promise me you'll stop running around the market, stealing food."

"I promise," Boiruch said.

Merie patted his head and smiled.

As another boy reported symptoms that indicated the disease, Merie herself began to feel sick. She went into the treasurer's room and asked him for two more matchboxes. After she had placed the specimens in them and wrapped them up, she placed them in her handbag, swung it over her shoulder, and didn't forget to gather up the empty infusion bottles to return to the hospital. She put on her flower-patterned dress she brought over from Rovno, which she mended after being severely torn.

Once again, she stood in line for the lab and when she reached the window, she put her hand in her bag to get the specimens, only to discover that the matchboxes weren't there. She stared in shock at the lab worker who was waiting for the specimens, and then again searched her bag. She recalled that at the last tram station, a stranger had pressed up close to her from behind as she felt that he put his hand in her bag. He got the matchboxes. She envisioned him unfolding the newspaper and discovering the contents of the matchboxes.

Merie burst out laughing uncontrollably sinking down on the pharmacy's floor. People around her thought she had lost her mind and two came up to her, but she pushed them away and stood up. She walked out of the hospital, still laughing, and to her surprise, noticed her stomach pains had stopped.

She decided to visit Etka at the Movement's apartment and entering the apartment, she burst out laughing again.

"Merie, what happened? I've never seen you laugh like that," Etka said.

"Forget it," Merie said, calming down.

"So, tell me," Etka continued, "what about joining the rail line to Samarkand?"

"I'm sorry but I can't do it," Merie replied. "Rafal is very busy with his new job at the archives, and I can't leave Alec for such a long time, and Ella won't take kindly to the idea. I'm really sorry."

"Too bad," Etka said. "We'll have to think of something else."

There was a knock at the door and Motak walked in. "Hello, sweet ladies," he said. "I'm glad to see you, Merie, I bring good tidings. I'm back from a meeting with the Polish consul, Mr. Kwampinski. I told him I'm forming a group of young Jewish men and women, members of the Hashomer Hatzair movement, who wish to join General Anders' Army and fight the Nazis. It turns out, he's familiar with our movement from the time he worked at the Polish Socialist Party in Warsaw. Anyway, he suggested we set up a meeting with the General and a few of the youngsters. But he also warned me that Anders is an anti-Semite, he hates Jews, he's from Poland's 'old school' and believes every Jew is a bloody Communist. So he warned me not to mention my connected with the Jewish movements' refugees, otherwise I'll most likely be kicked out of the room."

"And what if I join you for the meeting? I'm a registered experienced nurse."

"Didn't you hear what I just said? The man hates Jews, and your husband, my dear, is a Jew and a Communist, and to top it all, he holds a leading position in the Polish ZPP, the Union of Polish Patriots in Tashkent. And you want to talk to him to recruit you? And what about Rafal?"

"He's a big boy," Merie answered. "If he wants to stay in Russia and continue his activities in the ZPP, he'll stay. If he wants to join Anders' Army he'll have to leave them."

"That simple?" Motak asked.

"Yes," Merie replied. "If I have a chance to get to Palestine, I'll go with or without my husband."

"You're not only a Movement groupie, but you're also a Zionist," Motak chuckled.

"Yes, I am," Merie answered. "Tell me, did you ask about the orphanage?"

"As far as I know," Motak said, "the children in the convents will be joining Anders' Army. The only ones they'll leave behind are the adult Jews and Communists. It's interesting, that's exactly what the Nazis did when they invaded Poland."

"Maybe we can have some of our older children join the convents so that they too can leave with the Polish army?" Merie asked. "Can I come to the meeting?"

"I'd rather you didn't," Motak answered.

"Well, in that case," Merie said as she stood up, "I'll meet with him myself."

Chapter Twelve:
Clara

Merie headed straight to the National Hotel. The lobby was swarming with soldiers and civilians, all speaking Polish. She was surprised to see Clara at a table in the far corner of the lobby.

"Clara!" she called out. Spotting her, Clara stood up and hugged her warmly.

"When did you get to Tashkent?" Merie asked.

"Merie, I missed you so much. We've been here for months already, I got married and have a little girl, Anya, she's a year and a half old."

"Clara, that's wonderful!" Merie said. "We also have a son, Alec."

"We?" Clara asked.

"Clara, you were the one who introduced me to Rafal four years ago, in Warsaw."

"And you two have a son?" Clara wiped her tears. "Who'd have believed... there we were, before the war, sitting in a café in Warsaw, the pianist was playing a Chopin nocturne, and Rafal walked in and came over to say hello to me..."

"And then he gallantly kissed your hand and you introduced me, your best friend..."

"And here we are, in Tashkent," Clara said. "Unbelievable."

Merie told Clara she wished to meet with the consul and asked, "Are you also joining up with the Anders Army?"

"Yes, very soon," Clara said. "Apparently there's a list of Polish soldiers who fought the Germans. My husband was enlisted when the war broke out. But you can save yourself a lot of time," she added. "Kwampinski will send you to Anders, who once said that the Jews of Poland have the same privilege and duty as all other Poles to serve in the Polish army, and they should be trusted like all the other soldiers. But in fact, he's an anti-Semite and anti-Communist. If your husband is a Communist, they will not accept you. I heard also that the British don't want Jews to arrive with him to Palestine."

"Well, there you have it," Merie said.

"There are words and there are actions. Of course, the government doesn't want to be portrayed as discriminating against Jews, but in reality, it's doing everything in its power not to accept us. In our case, they had no choice, but Jews who weren't in the military before the war broke out, are rejected with all kinds of excuses."

"Well, I'm convinced that they need nurses. I'm going to try and talk with Kwampinski in any case."

Merie went up to the second floor. At the entrance to Kwampinski's office, an adjutant sat behind a desk. "Hello," Merie said "I'm a Polish nurse and I want to enlist in the army. I would like to speak to the consul."

"Well, then you'll have to go to the Polish army headquarters in Yangiyo'l and submit a request."

At that moment the office door opened and the consul stood there, bidding goodbye to a Polish nun. "Don't worry," he said. "We won't leave without the children. We won't leave you behind."

Merie tried to bypass the adjutant, but he blocked her way.

"This lady wants to speak with you, she wants to enlist in the army," he said.

"Did you tell her we don't handle recruitments?"

"I did, but..."

"Honorable sir," Merie began, "I'm a registered nurse with a great deal of experience from Czyste, in Warsaw. I'm sure you need my services."

"Excuse me, is the lady Jewish?" the Consul asked.

"Yes, Sir, I'm Jewish," Merie replied, "And a proud Polish woman."

"Please, tell me, is the lady married?"

"Yes, Sir, I'm married and we have a one-and-a-half-year-old son."

"Tell me, please, is the lady employed?"

"Yes, I work at the Jewish orphanage."

"Please, tell me, is the lady's husband employed?"

"Yes, Sir, he... he works at the Uzbekistan National Archives."

"Meaning, he's a Communist. Lady, please, if he weren't, he'd have no contact with the Archives."

"He is a Jewish refugee who is just trying to support his wife and son, your Honor."

"We can't enlist your husband, or take you and your son."

"Excuse me, Sir, what if I join the army without my husband? My son... he's eighteen months old..."

"Madame, will you be willing to leave your husband and embark on a journey of thousands of miles with an eighteen-month-old child?"

"Yes, Sir."

The Consul shook his head and asked, "Excuse me, madam, what's your name?"

"My name is Merie Gerber."

"Hear this, Mrs. Gerber. Our aim is to fight the Nazis, shoulder-to-shoulder with the British and the Americans, and we won't take anyone who isn't useful to us."

Merie put out her hand to the Consul. "Thank you for agreeing to talk with me," she said with tears in her eyes.

The Consul bowed slightly, and kissed her hand. "All the best to you and your son," he said.

Chapter Thirteen:
Teheran

Merie stormed into the orphanage and went directly to Ella's office. "Ella, I must talk to you, now," she said. Ella was sitting with Tanya, the kindergarten director, and the treasurer to discuss expanding the kindergarten facilities. "Not now," she said. "Don't you see we're having an important meeting?"

"Could you please give us a moment?" Merie asked. The treasurer looked at Tanya, bewildered, then they both stood up and left the room.

"You can't charge into my room like that and decide for me what's important or not," Ella said angrily, but with a slight smile on her lips.

"Ella, it is important," Merie said smiling. "I just heard that *Aliyat HaNoar* and other youth organizations are waiting in Teheran for children from the convents. They're setting up special camps for them there and will bring them to Eretz Yisrael, where Jewish families will adopt them. I went to the National Hotel to meet Kwampinski."

"To meet Kwampinski?"

"Yes, I want to escort the children, they'll need a nurse to look after them."

"But you're here, you're our nurse."

"You're right. My actions were spontaneous. I'm very worried, I'm... he refused my offer anyway. Ella, I think we should transfer the older children, like Boiruch and his gang, to the church orphanages, and send their names to Teheran, where they'll pull them out of the Polish army. That way, we'll be able to save some children away from this hellhole, and give them a chance for a future."

"So now you're involved in conspiracies?"

"It's their only chance to get out of here. And it will allow for more room here for younger children, which will lower food consumption. I'm sure the treasurer and Tanya will gladly accept what you call a conspiracy."

"You're right," Ella said. "I'm in contact with three Polish convent orphanages. I'll discuss this with our staff and we'll decide."

Merie gave her a kiss on her cheek. "You're great," she said.

As she headed to the family's room, she found Rafal watching Alec playing on the blanket spread out on the floor, which also served as their bed. Alec was holding an empty tin can, and Rafal put a few stones in it that rattled each time Alec moved it.

Rafal looked at Merie, questioningly, 'What now?' Merie was disappointed at not being accepted to Anders's Army and suddenly realized that Rafal was an obstacle in her way.

"I ran into Clara, from Warsaw, she sends her regards," she said.

"I know they're here in Tashkent, I ran into her and her husband too."

"You met them and didn't tell me? You know how close Clara and I were."

"When could I tell you? You're constantly running around fighting one epidemic after another."

Merie looked at him long and hard. "I saved this orphanage from the cholera epidemic, together with everyone else that put in the effort. I don't understand why you're belittling my work. If you met Clara, you certainly must know that they're joining Anders's Army on their way to Palestine."

115

"Yes, they told me. That's another reason why I didn't tell you I saw them. I know how badly you want to go and I didn't want to upset you."

"You're hiding things from me so as not to upset me? I want all of us to join Anders's Army."

"You know that's impossible," Rafal said. "And, please, keep your voice down."

"No! I'll shout so loudly that you and the entire orphanage will hear me." Alec stopped playing and looked at them.

Rafal stood up and took Merie in his arms as she burst into tears pounding his chest with her fists.

"Merie, the Anders Army is heading west as reinforcement for the British at El-Alamein to fight the Nazis. Egypt is nearly four hundred miles from Palestine. You insisted that we escape to Tashkent to distance ourselves from the Nazis."

"I'm fighting for our family, and I know that the best thing to do is to remove ourselves from the hunger in Russia," Merie said sobbing. "And you know very well that I'm not ready to go on living in fear of the NKVD! And I won't have our son grow up in a foreign land, where he'll be forced to live in constant fear!"

"When we were in Saratov, you refused to listen, and the same happened in Stalingrad, which you were right about then. You know Anders won't enlist me, and you also know that if the El-Alamein line falls, the Germans will invade Palestine within weeks. Wait a minute, where did you get all this information from?"

"I... I heard it from Etka," Merie said, her heart pounding from having lied to him.

Rafal roared out in anger, "You don't understand!"

"What don't I understand?" Merie yelled back.

Alec started crying and Merie picked him up, her tears mingling with his. "Look what we've done," she said. "We scared him."

"This isn't a matter of left or right," Rafal said. "If I apply to join the Anders Army, I will most likely end up with a bullet in my head, and maybe even in yours. And I'll tell you something else. The Russian army is using the National Archives to gather information and secret data. They discovered very quickly that I'm a professional archives director, and assigned me to check out data on all the generals commanding the army divisions that will be sent to the western front. So far, so good. But there's only one problem," Rafal smiled. "The Archives director can't read or write. He just signs his name."

"So how can he be the director of the National Archives?"

"Well, he's the brother of the Uzbekistan Party Secretary. So who then is actually running the Archives? His personal assistant, of course, namely, me. He signs all the excellent research reports and doesn't have a clue what's in them. And why am I telling you all this, Merie? So you'll understand that I, Rafal Gerber, am carrying a passport where it's clearly written, black on white, 'refugee from German occupied territory.' Which is like saying 'Half a Nazi spy.' Luckily for me, and for him, no one outside the Archives knows this. So, Merie, if I apply to the Anders Army and this reaches the Russian Secret Service, and most likely it will, I'll find myself in an NKVD interrogation room, and you know what that means."

Merie hugged Alec closely, rocking him gently from side to side. Any hopes she had of reaching Palestine with the Anders Army have vanished.

Chapter Fourteen:
Yangiyo'l, August 1942

The freezing winter gave way to the steaming Asiatic summer, together with the renewed fighting in the west. German forces rushed towards the Volga, targeting Stalingrad as their main goal. All around Tashkent, Russian troops were training before being sent to fight in the west. The crowds made it hard Rafal to get to the orphanage. He was working around the clock now, researching the officers allotted to command the forces being sent westward. He was also appointed as the head of the Union of Polish Patriots, an organization that was initiated with Stalin's blessings to help build Communist Poland.

At the Jewish orphanage, the process of transferring the older children to the Catholic convents had been completed. Boiruch, Shloimele, Yoel and all the other children who had recovered from cholera, were sent out, and Merie continued to visit them there.

"Here, sit down, have a cup of tea," Etka said as Merie entered after her last visit to the convent.

"I was so excited to see my boys on their way to our homeland," Merie said. "Tomorrow they're being transferred to the military camp at Yangiyo'l, and the day after that they'll be on their way to Teheran. I just wish I could join them."

"Well, you'll be glad to hear what I have to say," Etka began. "There's a rumor that a Polish colonel by the name of Rodnitski arrived here from Teheran, where he met with a Jewish Agency representative, and he's got a letter addressed to one Oscar Hendler, an activist in the Dror movement. Apparently, the letter contains a signed agreement between the Jewish Agency and the Polish army that lets the Poles send pioneers out of the Soviet Union. For three months now we've been searching for him in all the Polish camps throughout Central Asia."

As Merie returned to the orphanage, she told Ella she would be taking Alec to say goodbye to the older children leaving for Teheran. Ella studied Merie for a minute. "Are there any new ideas in that criminal mind of yours?" she asked with a smile. "You're sure it's a good idea to take an infant to Yangiyo'l? With you, even simple things become complicated. Whatever. You'll do what you want to in any case, but please, don't leave Russia without telling me."

"No...," Merie answered with a sly smile. "We're going to say goodbye. But that doesn't mean that my criminal mind hasn't considered an escape route." Merie kissed her and smiled. "In any case, I'll be grateful if this doesn't reach Rafal."

Merie was unable to fall asleep that night. Perhaps there will be a way she could get on one of the last trains going to Teheran? She loved Rafal, but lately they were fighting much more. She had lied to him. She was angry at his clinging to the Communist values, and was sure that otherwise, they both could have already reached Eretz Yisrael. Why did she lie to him? Why did she feel she needed to hide information from him? She remembered her promise to Ella not to leave without telling her. Is she really capable of leaving everything behind? She decided to write letters to Rafal and Ella, explaining her decision to get on one of those trains. If, for any reason, she will not manage to do that, she will tear up the letters when she returns from the train station.

In the early morning, Merie packed a knapsack with diapers, a clean change of clothes and food. She shouldered her handbag where she put some money and her passport, and headed for the train station. At the entrance, she met a group of the Hashomer Hatzair. Etka was there and embraced her. "It looks like you're going along with the children," she said. Merie smirked. I wish I really could get on the train with them, she thought to herself.

The train to Yangiyo'l entered the station, whistling loudly. Many platoons of Polish soldiers marched towards the train cars that awaited them, and a chain of military police prevented any civilians from getting close. At the other end of the platform, the soldiers' families waited to board. Jewish Polish refugees were demonstrating against the authorities that refused to recruit them to the Polish army, as well as prevented them from leaving the Soviet Union. The Polish military police confronted the demonstrators hitting them with their clubs to shove them away from the train.

In all the tumult, Shmuel, the Movement's liaison agent, suddenly noticed a tall Polish officer. "Excuse me, Sir, are you Colonel Rodnitski?" he quickly asked.

"Yes," the officer answered with surprise. "How do you know my name?"

"We are members of the youth movements Hashomer Hatzair and Dror, known as Hehalutz people. We've been looking for you for months. We understand you have a letter for Hendler that states that we can join you and even enlist to Anders Army."

"True," the colonel replied. "I have a letter. I expected Hendler to discuss things with me but so far I haven't met him."

"We're here," Shmuel said, "and we're ready to join up with this transport that's leaving."

"I'm willing to take all the members of Hehalutz on condition that within thirty minutes you can produce a list of their names and their passports. The list has to undergo inspection and get the approval of the Russian authorities before leaving."

Shmuel rushed to find his comrades, but could find no one except Merie. "Do you have a passport?" he called out to her.

"Yes. Why do you ask?" Shmuel quickly held her arm and pulled her after him to Colonel Rodnitski.

"I'm so sorry, Colonel. I couldn't find everyone in the little time I had. Only the two of us are here. I can show you documents that confirm I didn't live in the Soviet Union before the war."

Merie couldn't clearly make out what Shmuel and the colonel were saying. Will she be able to board the train with her son? Is her dream about to come true? And Rafal, what about him? He's about to lose not only his wife and son, but perhaps even his life. "I'm sorry," she said, "I won't be able to go on to Teheran."

An hour later, Shmuel found his friends and told them about the missed opportunity. Together they went in search of Colonel Rodnitski. When they approached him, he quickly said, "I'm sorry, it's now out of my hands. You're too late. I told you to come with the lists within thirty minutes."

"Yes, I know," Shmuel answered, "the train is leaving in just a few more minutes... at least can you consider taking on the few who are now here?"

"I'm sorry, the final passenger list is closed. This discussion is over. I will hand over to you the letter to Hendler. The last train leaves tomorrow morning. I will do my best to help you board that train." He turned his back to them and walked away.

The older children from the orphanage were wearing military uniforms that were too big for them. They were marched towards the train escorted by Polish sergeants. Merie waved to them, tears trickling down her cheeks, but her face shone with joy. At least these children are on the way to Eretz Yisrael.

"We're going back to Tashkent. There's nothing here anymore," Merie said to Etka.

The youth movements' members entered the train station, their faces clearly reflecting their disappointment. "Impossible," Motak murmured. "After months of searching, it's just not possible."

"If we could've gotten on the train, would you have come?" Etka asked Merie.

Merie nodded. "I prepared everything for leaving, but when I was asked to hand over my passport for the NKVD's approval, I pulled back, I couldn't do that to Rafal."

"I can't believe it... he doesn't know?"

"What you don't know can't hurt you... I left him a letter... now I'm going back to the orphanage to tear it up."

"Listen," Etka whispered, "we're lowering our heads closing down the apartment and dispersing. As of now, we are considered a dangerous organization and the NKVD is on our tracks. Three of our members have recently been caught, one of them was tortured in one of the NKVD's secret basements. I suggest you break all contact with us for the next few months."

Merie nodded in agreement.

"But what about you?" she asked.

"Motak and I are heading for Samarkand. We'll try to keep our heads down, and when the pressure is off, sometimes in the future, I'll contact you."

When Merie reached the orphanage, she rushed to their room. Rafal was sitting at the rickety table, holding her letter in his hand. His face was pale, disappointment, depression and anger written all over it.

"Were you planning to leave for Teheran with Alec without telling me?" he shouted at her.

Merie put Alec down on the blanket. Crouching near Alec, she turned to Rafal. "I'm sorry, this should never have happened."

"You were going to leave for Palestine, with Alec, that's what you wrote in this letter! Not only were you planning to leave me, but you also put my life in danger!"

"I'm sorry."

Rafal opened his passport to the second page and pointed to it. "Do you know what it means being 'a refugee from German occupied territory'? I told you, they could arrest me and worse, and yet you went ahead and put me in danger, yourself and our son, with your dreams of Palestine. Do you want us to separate? Do you even love me?"

Merie began to sob. "It has nothing to do with my loving you, you're my husband, the father of my child, and I'll cut off my contact with my friends from the Hashomer Hatzair. But as I told you, I don't want my child growing up in a strange land, under a frightening, tyrannical regime. Yes, I tried to join the Anders Army. I believed that if Clara could do it, so could I. Please forgive me."

Rafal remained sitting, not moving. Then he stood up and pulled her up from the blanket. He kissed her with tears rolling down his cheeks.

Chapter Fifteen:
David Perlmutter

1943. It was a clear February winter day. The skies were blue and the temperature dropped below zero. Merie was at the orphanage on her way to the infirmary, when she ran into Pola, the counselor in charge of the older children.

Twice a week Pola would go to the train station and carefully observe the crowd rushing by on the platforms, scouting for abandoned children who got off the trains and would bring them to the orphanage.

"Any new arrivals this morning?" Merie asked.

"Two, they were filthy. I sent them to wash up. When they're done, they'll come to you to be examined."

In walked the first young lad. He had on clothes from the orphanage and a grey cap on his head. Merie asked him his name, but he didn't answer. He looked at her suspiciously and quickly glanced around the infirmary. Merie was used to the distrustful behavior of children new to the orphanage, and again gently repeated her question. The boy remained silent. Merie placed a slice of dark bread on the table and asked, "Are you hungry?" The boy nodded. "Answer a few questions and then you could eat. What's your name?"

"David Perlmutter."

"Where are you from?" Again, silence. Merie knew that David was debating whether to trust her. "Dear boy," she said, "I need to know something about you so I can help you."

"I came from the fascist side," David answered, "from Pinsk."

Merie dropped her pen and stared at him with eyes wide open. Since leaving left Rovno, she had never met any refugees from Pinsk. She felt a slight pressure in her chest.

"How old are you, David?"

"Fourteen."

"Please take off your coat, your shirt, and your boots," she said. "You have nothing to be afraid of. Every child who comes here gets a physical checkup."

The boy shrugged. Merie smiled at him and said, "Dear boy, it's my job to make sure you stay healthy. How can I do that if I don't check you first?"

David stared into space, then began taking off his clothes. He was very skinny with his ribs protruding, due to his severe malnutrition and his hands, legs and face were covered with scratches. Merie completed his physical examination, which proved that despite David's extreme thinness, he was in general good health. She told him to put his clothes back on, prepared two cups of tea and invited him to join her. She then handed him the bread, which he eagerly devoured and then once again lowered his eyes to the ground. Merie smiled and put out her hand to him, but he cringed from her touch.

"Drink your tea," she said, adding, "I too am from Pinsk."

David looked up at her. "You're from Pinsk? When did you leave?"

"Years ago," she said, "but I studies at the *Tarbut* Gymnasia in Pinsk so consider myself a 'Pinsker.'"

"Well, then, you and me, we're the last of the Jews from Pinsk," David whispered.

"What?" Merie exclaimed.

"The Pinsk we knew no longer exists. The Germans killed everyone. All the Jews."

Merie shook her head in disbelief. "But there were tens of thousands of Jews there," she said.

"There were..."

Tears began running down her cheeks. "Tell me everything, please."

"About a year-and-a-half ago, in the summer, the Germans entered the city," David began. "First, they caught a bunch of Jews out on the street and told them they're taking them to work but the next day they killed them. They set up a Jewish administration that they called Judenrat, and the man chosen to direct it was David Alper, who was principal of the *Tarbut* Gymnasia."

"David Alper? He was my teacher, I liked him so much," Merie said.

"He headed the Judenrat for only two days. Then he quit when he realized that his job was just to rat on the Jews to the Germans. Then, two days later, was the first *Actsia* and David Alper was also selected. After that *Actsia*, the only thing that interested the Germans was to rob the Jews for gold, furs and clothing. The furs were the most important and the families which had furs were all hanged." David continued talking in a dry, apathetic tone, as if what he was saying had nothing to do with him.

"Then, they planned to drown all of us in the swamps outside the city and ordered all the women and children to march there, but the water only reached up to our knees, so we returned to the city."

"Who did they want to drown?"

"They ordered every male from the age of fourteen to sixty to report for work. In order to make sure everyone showed up, they arrested three hundred men and said they would kill them all if the others didn't show up. The next day, all the men and young boys showed up at the town square and were sent out to work." David stopped his flow of words, needing to gather his strength to go on. "After walking for a few miles, they reached a clearing where the Germans had dug huge holes in the ground. They were ordered to undress and lie down in the holes and then the Germans shot them. Anyone who tried to escape was shot down by German horsemen who kept guard around the area. Only two tried to escape and the Germans forced young boys to drag their bodies to the holes. Those boys... some were my friends," David said. "They covered the holes with earth and then they too were killed. Besides doctors and other needed professions, women and children, all the Jewish men were killed."

Merie looked at him, shocked. "All of them?"

"All of them."

"Go on," she said.

"Later on, for the next few months there weren't any more *Actsias*, and the Jews that remained, especially the women and children, worked for the Germans. Then all the Jews that were left were forced to enter a ghetto."

"A ghetto? In Pinsk?"

"They took a number of streets, built barbed wire fences around them and forced all the Jews from the nearby towns and villages to move into that ghetto. It was terribly crowded, hunger and diseases prevailed.

On our way to the ghetto, the Germans stood at every street corner together with the Polish mob that jeered and yelled at us to move on, while snatching the packs from our backs that held all our possessions, and took out everything they wanted.

As fall came, we were afraid they were going to destroy the entire ghetto. I knew some ways of sneaking out since I used to secretly go over to the Polish side to bring food for the family.

Mother told me it was too dangerous to stay in the ghetto, but I wanted to stay with her and my sisters," David continued in a broken voice. "But Mother insisted that I go and join the partisans out in the woods near the bogs. 'Tell them your father fought with the Red Army. That way they won't kill you, and try to move east, look for your father.'"

"So how did you manage to escape from the ghetto?"

"One night, I crawled under the fence. All the streets around the ghetto were dark and I managed to reach the bogs. I was familiar with them. My father's job was to manage the forest rangers and the other workers in the forests and the bogs around Pinsk. I knew the paths that led to the parts in the forest the Germans didn't enter, being afraid they'll sink in the bogs. That's where I met the partisans."

David then picked up the teacup and sipped quietly. "After a few days," he continued, "a partisan showed up and told us that the Germans surrounded the ghetto. They took young boys to dig holes outside the city, then led all the Jews out of the ghetto to these holes and shot them all. Then they forced the diggers to cover the holes and finally shot them too. Only two buildings were left and at the beginning the Germans housed a few especially skilled Jews se in them, whom they needed, keeping them in a sort of small ghetto, but later I heard that it too was destroyed."

The infirmary fell silent. Merie couldn't stop her tears, while David's eyes remained dry. He had already seen everything.

"When you were in the woods, did you hear anything about Horodno and Stolin?"

"Yes," David said. "I met two people from Stolin. They said the Germans built a ghetto there too, and sent all the Jews from the nearby towns there. They killed everyone in the ghetto even before they totally destroyed the ghetto in Pinsk. There were maybe thirty people who managed to escape to the woods... I know they tried to organize an underground group in the ghetto to fight the Nazis, but in the end, like in Pinsk, there wasn't any resistance."

Merie caught her head between her hands. "My entire world, the world I knew, is gone," she said with tears flowing down her cheeks. "Maybe you heard of my brother, Gadi, or Gudel, Hackman? Maybe you ran into him?"

"No," David answered. "I didn't run into him, but maybe he joined up with the groups in the forests. The forests became the partisans' kingdom."

"So how did you end up in Tashkent?" Merie asked wiping away her tears.

"I kept moving eastward for a few months, from one partisan group to another, in order to reach the Russian forces spread along the Volga River. Crossing the Dnieper River was extremely dangerous, but we swam across at night. Finally, near Kharkov, the partisans handed me over to the Russian forces. I could find my father, the soldiers had no time to look after me and so eventually I ended up in Saratov where I heard about Tashkent. I decided to take a train through Kazakhstan. The trains were pretty empty so it wasn't hard to find a seat."

Merie gazed at the thin boy who had just told her of the destruction of her town about most likely was her family's bitter end.

Merie was restless all night long, she dreamt of smashed violins, of deep open holes in the ground that swallowed her and Alec up. "Rafal!" she screamed, "save the boy!"

Rafal held her closely trying to calm her down. The following morning, Merie stayed together with Rafal. Again and again, she repeated David's words and mourned her parents' death. "I could have fought for them. I could have forced them to leave!"

"You did the best you could, Merie, I'm sure."

"And what about Gudel? Maybe he escaped. Maybe he's together with the partisans? How am I going to find my dear brother...," she sobbed bitterly. "And my mother, and Father!"

"Mo-mmy," Alec murmured. Merie stood up. "Did he just say 'Mommy?'"

Chapter Sixteen:
The Wounded Man
From Stalingrad

The following morning Merie decided to return to work. In the infirmary, she treated a little boy with an injured knee as a messenger from the Central Hospital in Tashkent knocked and opened the infirmary door. "Are you Merie Gerber?" he asked.

"Yes. Who wants to know?"

"I was sent by the head nurse of the Central Hospital. She wants to meet with you as soon as possible."

"What could Ludmila possibly want with me?" Merie asked as she continued bandaging the child's knee.

"I don't know," the messenger replied. "I was told to tell you that it's urgent."

Merie looked at the messenger and said, "Tell Ludmila that I'll meet her at the hospital at four o'clock this afternoon."

Merie sent the little boy back to his class, cleaned the instruments she had used and put them away, and headed to Ella's office.

"Merie, so sorry to hear! My condolences."

Merie nodded. "I refuse to believe that they're gone," she said. "But life is calling me, and so is the future, and I'll look for Gudel, maybe he managed to survive. Ella, thanks for your kind words, but if I continue thinking about my parents, I won't be able to continue with my chores. A messenger just arrived from the Central Hospital inviting me to a meeting with the head nurse. He told me she said it's urgent. Do you know anything about this?"

"No..." Ella shrugged.

"Maybe they think we owe them something, since they helped us during the epidemic."

"I hope they don't decide to take you away from us," Ella said.

At three o'clock Merie went to their room to change, then took Alec to the nursery schoolteacher, "Rafal is supposed to pick up Alec at five. If he doesn't show up, then please watch him for me till I return."

At four o'clock, Merie knocked on the door of the head nurse's office. "Hello, Ludmila," she said.

"Hello, Merie. Please, come in and sit down," Ludmila pointed to the chair opposite her. "Would you like something to drink?" Merie politely declined. "I'm sure you're aware of the recent battles around Stalingrad," Ludmila continued. "The wounded are being sent to makeshift hospitals along the eastern bank of the Volga River."

"Yes, I heard," Merie answered.

"it's been decided to send the soldiers that need long rehabilitation to Tashkent. So they've set up a tent hospital here in Tashkent with the help of the American army equipment and doctors and nurses. I really need you," Ludmila said. "We desperately need nurses. Nurses that can take charge of a tent with sixty wounded soldiers and help them get through the night. I know you have a two-year-old son and you're responsible for the care of the children at the orphanage, but I need you to come and work two nights a week."

"You've taken me by surprise," Merie said. "You know, my husband works day and night at the Central Archives and I'm busy with my responsibilities at the orphanage. But I'll speak with Ella, the director, and see what we can do."

"Merie, I'm sorry, I didn't invite you here to consult with you, but to tell you that you have to report tomorrow at five p.m. to the hospital, at tent number fifteen."

"I'll relay what you've said to Ella and I'll be there," Merie said as she stood up to leave.

At five o'clock the following afternoon, Merie, in the white nurse's uniform Ludmila gave her, arrived at the hospital. The grounds were covered in large white tents with red crosses on their side flaps. Merie looked for tent number fifteen, where she was told to report to.

The doctor in charge asked her about her experience and together they entered the tent. Inside the tent, sixty beds were arranged in two long rows, and at its far end, a table and chair served as the nurses' station.

"The sixty wounded soldiers here suffer from injuries of various degrees of severity," the doctor explained. "At night, we don't treat them, they are all stabilized. If there is a patient whose condition suddenly turns worse, pressing the emergency button will immediately bring in a doctor and an emergency team. Every day, between five and five-thirty p.m., there is an overlap with the morning nurse.

"How many tents like this are there here at the hospital?" Merie asked.

"Fifty. There are three thousand wounded patients here. This field hospital was set up with the help of the Americans, who financed and provided all the equipment, from the beds to the surgery rooms, and even the staff dining hall. You will be get a full nutritious meal which are also provided by the Americans."

After reviewing the clipboards attached to each of the beds with details about the wounded patients, the doctor took his leave. As night fell, Merie sat down at the nurses' station and turned on the table lamp. She was suddenly overwhelmed with anxiety. Years had passed since she was responsible for the lives of so many severely wounded. She recalled the doctor's words, "Don't be afraid. I have been here for three months and so far no nurse has died while on duty."

Every hour, Merie walked past every bed and read once again the patients' names.

"Nurse, can you please bring me some water?" a soldier with his face bandaged asked.

"Of course," Merie replied.

"My name is Ivan Alexandrovitch Michlin," the soldier said, "I'm an officer from Stalingrad."

"You fought in Stalingrad, Ivan?" she asked.

"Yes, ma'am, I was an artillery officer. We fought in the ditches on the front line. I used a landline to direct the artillery...," the soldier replied and moaned.

Merie rearranged his pillow and returned to her desk. She then heard someone faintly calling out, "Nurse... nurse..."

The clipboard on his bed carried his name – Vasili Morozov, and his condition – a double leg amputee. "Did you call me, Vasili?" she asked quietly.

"Yes, nurse. My legs hurt." Merie looked at his two stumps and realized his were phantom pains she had studied about in Warsaw, and yet she gave him a pill to ease his pain.

"Thank you, nurse," Vasili said. "Could you please sit here with me for a little while?"

Merie drew her chair up to his bed and sat down. "Where are you from, Vasili?"

"Siberia. With the 284th Siberian Division," he smiled and then immediately turned sullen. "Because of the fascists..."

"How were you wounded, Vasili?" Merie asked. "What was your position?"

"I am a sniper. We were stationed in Stalingrad to protect the city and after we crossed the Volga in early October, we set up camp in the ruins of an old tractor factory. It was the perfect place for us snipers to hide and shoot from. We were instructed to shoot only at officers. Did you ever hear of Zichev and Chekhov?"

"They were with the 13th Guardia Division, weren't they? I read about them in the papers."

"They became great heroes! But our Tanya Chernova shot eighty Germans single-handedly! I made do with half that number," he chuckled. "What happened was that at the end of November, there was an air attack on the factory. And, here, see, my two legs were trapped under huge cement blocks. My comrades continued on to their next mission, they said they'd come back to take me to a central converging point... but no one returned. Who knows, maybe they were all killed. Well, I had no choice. I managed to free myself from under the cement blocks and then crawled to the river, to the converging point. I crawled for two days! Lucky for me, we Siberians are men of steel, we know how to survive!" Vasili smiled. "Now I'm hoping they'll fit me with prostheses and I'll be able to stand on my legs again."

Merie placed her hand gently on his forehead. "Try to sleep. You will need all your strength."

"You know, nurse," Vasili whispered, "there were so many dead... and what were we, we were..."

"You were what?" Merie asked.

"In Siberia," Vasili smiled, "when a pack of wolves attacked our goatherds, we would tie a goat to a tree, then we'd lie in wait a few yards away. Then the wolves would show up, surround the goat and we'd shoot down every single one of them.

The same thing happened in Stalingrad... we were placed in the remains of what was once Stalingrad, in order to draw out the finest German soldiers, who surrounded us from all sides... I hope," Vasili murmured, "that all this suffering was worth it..."

Once again, Merie stroked his forehead, then carried her chair back to the nurses' station and thought about Alec. He was taking his first steps. What kind of a world awaits him, a world filled with war and sorrow?

Chapter Seventeen:
The Union Of Polish Patriots

Day after day, month after month, Merie was busy at the orphanage, looking after Alec, and doing her shifts at the hospital. Rafal was occupied with the National Archives of the Uzbekistan nation and with the ZPP – the Union of Polish Patriots that struggled against the Polish government-in-exile seated in London, being the kernel of a new to be-established Polish government, backed by the Communist Soviet Union.

As July drew to a close, the wounded soldiers from Stalingrad in the field hospital were replaced with the wounded from the Battle of Kursk. Then, in the early months of 1944, these were replaced with the wounded from the battles in the Ukraine. In February, Rovno was liberated and four months later, the hospital once again received the wounded from that battle too.

One morning, there was a knock on the infirmary door and there stood Etka, with two men by her side. Two years had passed since she and Merie parted ways at the train station.

"Etka!" Merie cried. "I didn't know you're back in Tashkent." The two women hugged for a long moment.

"I came back with Yisrael and Shlomo. They're leaders of the Movement in the east and they wanted me to set up a meeting with Rafal."

"With Rafal!" Merie has asked surprised.

"Yes, we're interested in joining the Vanda Army," Yisrael said.

"The Vanda Army is a division organized by the Union of Polish Patriots in Lublin, headed by Wanda Wasilewska. They want to fight alongside the Russian army," Shlomo explained. "And Rafal is one of the leaders here of the Union of Polish Patriots."

"You want to fight the Nazis, after the Russians rejected your request to enlist in the Red Army?"

"First of all, we want to find out who of our friends from *Hashomer Hatzair* in Vilna, Pinsk, Bialystok and Rovno are still alive. Then we can pursue the options for making *aliyah* to *Eretz Yisrael*. So far, we've learned that will be very difficult."

"I will talk to him this evening," she said. "As to making *aliyah*, I'll spare him that part. I'll tell him you're interested in joining the Vanda Army and meeting up with whoever of our friends survived the war. Etka, call Ella's office tomorrow and I'll have an answer for you."

In the evening, Rafal returned to their room and picked up Alec. Like all the children at the orphanage, Alec too was very thin, for lack of nourishment. Although food rations have increased in the past few months, thanks to the Americans, everyone suffered from malnutrition and weight loss, including Rafal.

Merie poured Rafal a bowl of steaming soup from the pot standing on a kerosene burner in the corner. "I found some cabbage in the market right near the orphanage," Merie said. "We're celebrating."

They sat at the table to eat the soup, along with the three slices of bread rationed to them. When they finished, Merie said, "Today, I had a visitor. Etka came to see me, and with her were two Movement activists. They want to meet with you."

"Meet with me? What've I got to do with the *Hashomer Hatzair*? You know I want nothing to do with them, ever since that episode with the Anders Army."

"But this isn't about the Anders Army, it's about the Vanda Army," Merie smiled at him.

"What's their connection to the Vanda Army? They want to join a Communist division of the Russian army?"

"Yes, that's how I understood it."

Rafal snickered. "They really want to join the Vanda Army or maybe they're trying to leave Tashkent under the protection of the Union of Polish Patriots?"

The following evening, Etka, Yisrael and Shlomo arrived, accompanied by another friend, Tuvia. The meeting was held in the dining hall of the orphanage, which at that hour stood empty. Rafal welcomed them and said, "Who would have believed that in a small dining hall in a Jewish orphanage in Tashkent a summit meeting is being held between *Hashomer Hatzair*'s Asian leadership and leaders of Asia's Union of Polish Patriots. So tell me, what brings you here?"

"We're a group of Jewish Polish Socialists who wish to join the Vanda Army," Shlomo began. "We heard that the Polish division is organizing in Lublin."

"When the Anders Army was recruiting, you wanted to join the army under the leadership of the government-in-exile in London. What were you then? Weren't you Zionists?"

The comrades got angry and stood up to leave. Rafal raised his hand and said, "Calm down. I know who you are and what you represent. What is it that you really want?"

"To reach Lublin," Yisrael answered quietly, "and look for our friends who were left behind."

"That's much better," Rafal smiled. "If you insist on enlisting in what's called the Vanda Army, well, the leadership has no interest in the army and the new government in Lublin being perceived as Jewish, and therefore the Vanda Army isn't interested in recruiting Jews. You might as well forget about it. And if you quote me, I'll deny that I ever said this."

"And what if we are looking to find our friends in the west?" Tuvia asked.

"Well, you're not the only ones and there's another solution to that."

"What other solution?" They asked.

"It has to do with money, a great deal of it. And, again, everything I'm about to say will be denied if any of you ever quote me," Rafal said and looked intently at the foursome waiting for his explanation.

"We understand," Shlomo said, "we swear we won't mention a word of this conversation."

"There are some Poles," Rafal continued, "you can call them wheeler-dealers, who produce forged documents with Polish names. With these documents, you can go to the Soviet municipal officer in Tashkent and ask to be recruited as experts for the government in Lublin. But, this costs money. The municipal officer forms a group to which he attaches a Russian army officer as an escort. This officer is chosen from the numerous wounded soldiers who arrived here after the recent battles in the west, and are no longer fit for combat, and he too gets paid."

"I have just the right officer for this," Merie jumped in. "His name is Ivan Alexandrovitch Michlin. He's an injured soldier I took care of. He has stayed behind in the hospital and is helping me look after the wounded. We've become friends and he'll do anything I ask."

"The entire chain that I mentioned," Rafal went on, "starting from the wheeler-dealer who prepares the documents, the municipal officer's approval, and the escorting officer – all this comes at a very high price."

No one spoke for a moment. "Do you have any idea how much it would cost to send an emissary to the west through this system?" Shlomo asked.

"I believe about three thousand rubles will cover the cost of this chain. I'll give you the name of a certain Polish man, contact him, but don't ever mention my name."

Again everyone fell silent. Yisrael stood up and shook Rafal's hand, as did Shlomo and Tuvia.

"We're grateful to you, Rafal," Yisrael said. "I promise you, in the name of all of us here, our word of honor, that this meeting never took place. Merie, we'll be in touch with you regarding Ivan Alexandrovitch, when we get to that point."

Etka hugged Merie and the four left and disappeared into the darkness of the night.

The following day, when Rafal returned home, he asked Merie for a word.

"You seem very happy," Merie said. "What happened?"

"Listen," he said. "The war is coming to an end. Our government has been established in Lublin and an embassy was set up in Moscow. Today I was told that I'm going to be appointed secretary of the Polish Embassy in Moscow. The director of the National Archives received a request to release me from my present position."

Merie looked at him, leaned over the table separating them, and kissed his lips. "Moscow? The hunger is ending? We'll be able to sleep in a real bed on a mattress, and have a normal life?"

Rafal smiled and held her hand. "It looks like you can inform the orphanage and the hospital that by the end of November, early December, we'll be in Moscow. I'll be going there next month to prepare for your arrival."

"Rafal," Merie said and burst into tears, "since little David told me about Pinsk, I keep dreaming about Mother and Father. How can I find out what happened to them?"

3.

MOSCOW 1944

Chapter One:
The Road To Moscow

It was mid-December and freezing cold in Tashkent. Rafal had left four months earlier and every week he and Merie would talk on the phone in Ella's office. On the day Merie was to leave Tashkent, she packed all their possessions in one suitcase she had bought in the market. She went to the nursery school and took her leave from every child, hugging each one. She could not hold back her tears. The train to Moscow was leaving in the afternoon.

Merie entered Ella's office. The orphanage staff had gathered there to say goodbye. They held up glasses filled with water. "Usually we'd raise a glass of wine in such situations," Ella began, "but we'll make do with life-sustaining water. To you, Merie. You are a superb nurse and so many children are alive today thanks to you. Don't forget us in Moscow."

Merie hugged them, and said, "You were my family for the worst part of this damned war. I am beginning my journey back to my husband, heading west. In the future, when a new nation will be established in *Eretz Yisrael*, I will be there. Thanks again."

She left the orphanage compound holding Alec's hand in one hand and their suitcase in the other. A taxi was waiting outside to take them to the train station – a parting gift from Ella.

Merie was directed to the first-class train car. To her amazement, she found herself in a cabin with a comfortable couch as well as two beds: the upper berth for her, the lower for Alec. The dining car was open for her, where they served hot meals.

The transition from the itchy blanket spread out on the packed earth at the orphanage, to a double-deck bed on the train was hard for her to swallow. Alec sat on the couch and played with a soft ball, a gift from the nursery. The dress Merie was wearing was so faded and worn, she suddenly felt a great contrast between her appearance and the other passengers' attire. She hugged Alec close and said, "Alechico, we're going to Dad."

"Where is Dad?" Alec asked.

"In Moscow. We'll get therein a week. Meanwhile, this will be our lovely home."

"Why?" the child asked innocently.

"Why is he in Moscow? He's the secretary of the Polish Embassy. Your father is a historian who's in charge of cultural matters."

"Why?"

"Why is he a historian? That's a good question. I never asked him."

"Why is Dad in Moscow?"

"We're beginning our journey back home. We're going home, Alechico."

"To Moscow?"

"Moscow is just a step on our way home. We are Jews, Alechico, and we need a land of our own. Once Poland was home, but after this war, it's no longer."

"So where is our home?"

"You're asking some tough questions, Alechico. Palestine is home. It is our *Eretz Yisrael*. It isn't ours yet..."

"So we're going to a home that isn't ours?"

"We're on a train to Moscow now. What happens later, we'll wait and see."

"And I'll be in kindergarten there like in Tashkent?"

"Yes, Alechico. You're going to go to kindergarten and meet new friends in Moscow."

"What language will the children talk there?"

"Just like at the orphanage in Tashkent. Some will talk Polish, others will talk Russian."

"And in the land where our home is, do they also speak Polish and Russian?"

Merie burst out laughing. "In the land where our home is they speak Hebrew."

"Do you speak Hebrew?" the child asked.

"Yes. When I was a young girl, I studied Hebrew. I speak Hebrew with Etka from *Hashomer Hatzair* and her friends. Now let's go to the dining car. It's time for lunch."

The train kept moving towards Moscow. The days passed, and once in a while the train would stop for several days to clear the tracks for trains going west, laden with soldiers and military equipment headed for the battle to conquer Warsaw and Poland. Merie felt secure. The Germans had been pushed back and victory was near. The sight of demolished homes was seen everywhere along the tracks, as were burnt tanks, capsized trucks, and firearms that hadn't been collected yet. The military's main thrust and focus was to push forward to Berlin.

After ten days on the train, in the early morning, the train entered the Kazansky Station in Moscow. There, on the platform, stood Rafal, wearing a long black coat and holding a bouquet of red roses.

Chapter Two:
The Baltschug Hotel

The Baltschug Hotel was their first home in Moscow. It was situated on the edge of the Red Square, opposite the Soviet Parliament, the Duma, where some of the Polish party leaders and the embassy staff were living.

Their family's room at the Baltschug Hotel on the first floor was spacious. In one corner stood a large brown closet that could contain several times the quantity of all their possessions. Next to it was a child's bed and in the opposite corner stood a double bed, and a round table with four chairs in the middle of the room. Although the bathroom and kitchen were jointly used by all the tenants on the floor, in contrast to their Tashkent experience this was a tremendous step up.

Merie found herself gazing at the bed on which several dresses were spread out, along with new underwear, shirts and shoes. "Rafal," she said, "where does all this bounty come from? I see there are also clothes here for Alec... and dresses. It's all for us?"

Rafal smiled. "Yes. I knew you'd arrive dressed in the old clothes from Tashkent. This city is unlike what you have been used to. Here in Moscow we'll no longer want for anything and won't eat soup with bread. I knew you would need new clothes and matching shoes, so I got help from Danote, who you will meet later on. I asked her to see to your wardrobe. You had better throw out all your and Alec's old clothes and I'll be happy to have you meet the wives of our party members. They're all waiting in the lobby of the Moscow Hotel. They know you're supposed to arrive and are looking forward to greeting you."

"I'd love to," Merie said, "but what about Alechico?"

"Well, if you agree, I've already arranged a young lady from the hotel to watch him. Anyhow, he'll soon fall asleep."

Merie looked at Rafal. "You really thought of everything," she said and spread out a tailored dress on the bed.

"Danote has pretty good taste," she smiled putting her arms around his neck. Rafal kissed her fervidly. "I missed you," she said, "and so did Alechico. We missed you so much."

"I know. I also missed you terribly, my darling wife. Every night I thought about you, it's very cold here in Moscow." Merie embraced Rafal longingly, as Alec appeared at their side.

"Mom," he said, "look at my bed! No one in the nursery has a bed like mine. Can I sleep in it today and tomorrow too?"

"Of course you can. It's just for you," Rafal said.

Alec quickly took off his shoes and Merie watched as he began jumping up and down on the bed, then finally lay down and shut his eyes.

Rafal and Merie walked across the bridge that led to Red Square. They crossed the square and entered the Moscow Hotel. The embassy wives were sitting around a low table in the lobby, to which they both headed.

"This is my wife, Merie, she just arrived this morning from Tashkent," Rafal said with a smile. She's not just my wife, she's an expert nurse in childcare and worked in a field hospital for wounded soldiers. I'll leave you ladies alone. I'm sure you'll be able to guide her and share your expertise with her."

"Rafal, go on, go take care of cultural things," Sonia said, "and leave Merie to us. Don't worry, she's in good hands. Merie, come join us. Tell us about your trip here with your son. What's his name?"

"His name is Alec," Merie said, "and compared to our life in Tashkent, the train was a luxury hotel. We even enjoyed hot meals, and yet, you surely can imagine that ten days with a three-year-old in a small cabin is never easy."

"Olga has a four-year-old girl and my son is three, so Alec will have friends," Danote said. "But most important is to show Merie how to live here in Moscow. I suggest we take her on a tour of our exclusive shop. Did Rafal give you the entry card to Moscow's Garden of Eden?" She asked and everyone burst out laughing. "What it means is that you can shop in this place that's only for the political elite and the families of foreign embassies. You can buy food, clothing and other items that cannot be found anywhere else in Moscow. Sadly, for us, we have to make do with this Soviet shop. At one time, we were able to shop in the American supermarket as well, that was run by the American Embassy and offered a far greater variety of items, but the Russian disapproved. Don't worry, your account will be charged to the embassy. I suggest we get to the store and you'll see what we're talking about. First, you need to buy one or two dresses for everyday wear, as well as an evening dress. We're invited with our husbands to many functions. But most important, you have to have a very good coat because the Moscow winters are cruel. By the way, I see you're wearing a dress I picked out for you. It's lovely on you."

"Thank you, Danote, for your effort. Your choices were obviously made with great care. I'll be happy to buy several new dresses and a warm coat. But I'll also need to buy some warm clothes for Alec. And also, I need to fill up the pantry in our room, so I can cook a good meat soup for the family."

"So ladies, what are we waiting for?" Sonia said.

"I'm sorry I won't be able to join you," Olga said. "There's a meeting at the Czech Embassy to which I have to accompany my husband. But I know you'll be excellent escorts for Merie. I'll be glad to join you on the next shopping spree."

The women stepped out of the hotel into the snow-covered street. Despite the sun and blue skies, the air was piercingly cold. At the entrance to the shop, the women's documents were carefully inspected from which they entered a large hall. Merie had never seen such a shop in Warsaw before the war, and certainly never in Rovno or Tashkent. To the right was a large food section with a butchery with excellent meats, a special section with exclusive cheeses and milk products, shelves with a variety of breads and baked goods, and long shelves filled with cans of foods and other food items, and kitchen utensils. Merie felt dizzy. "I never knew such a thing existed..." she murmured.

"Forget that," Sonia said, "first you have to pick out some new clothing, and then we'll go back to the food department."

Merie was led to the women's clothing department sporting long aisles full of dresses, blouses and trousers. She chose two woolen dresses for everyday wear and a long sapphire-blue evening dress. She chose a pair of warm boots and one pair of elegant shoes for evening wear. For Alec, Merie picked out two sets of clothing and a warm coat. At the food section, she picked up whatever she could find. "How am I going to drag all this back to the hotel?" She felt a bit ridiculous.

"We'll help you put it all in a cab that will take you to the hotel. I'm sure Rafal gave you some rubles for the driver."

Merie smiled. "To tell you the truth, I need to get used to such a change."

"We've all been through this," Danote said. "The embassy was set up here only four months ago and before that we lived in Saratov and Kuybyshev under similar conditions. Believe me, it's easy to get used to this lifestyle."

On Saturday, several days later, Rafal returned to the hotel carrying a wooden snow sled. He looked out the window at the grey skies and then at Merie. "Alec," he said, "get dressed warmly, with warm pants and shirt, your boots, gloves and woolen hat, and your earmuffs."

"Yay! Yay!" Alec cried.

"Be back by two o'clock." Merie said. "I'll have meat soup and potatoes waiting for you."

Rafal and Alec tied a long rope to the snow sled and went out to Alexander Park, first crossing the great bridge over the Moscow River, and then the Red Square. They reached the Kremlin's Clock Tower when the clock hands were on eleven a.m.

"You know, Alechico," Rafal said, "Comrade Stalin is sitting at his desk now looking out on the Red Square. When he sees you, he'll ring the bell so you'll know he was looking at you. Do you want Comrade Stalin to see you?"

"Yes," said Alec. He stood in the middle of the square just as the bell of the clock banged. Alec's jaw dropped with amazement.

"See?" Rafal said, smiling. "Comrade Stalin saw you, just like I promised."

Alexander Park was filled with children and their parents who were sliding down the hill to the frozen river.

"Here, let me show you how," Rafal said. He held Alec's hand pulling the rope as they climbed up a short incline. At the top, he sat Alec down on it and told him, "As long as your legs are in the air, you'll sledge. If you want to stop, stick the heels of your boots in the snow. Got it?"

Alec for the first time, down to the bottom of the hill and stopped. From that day the sled became his best friend throughout the winter. He took it with him wherever he went. One day, while with the babysitter, he snuck out of the room with the sled in his hands, and went to Alexander Park. When

Merie returned and asked the babysitter, a neighbor's daughter, where he was, she started crying mumbling, "I don't know where he disappeared to."

Merie searched throughout the hotel and then ran to the kindergarten that was closed that day. She called the embassy's security guard, who called the police. As Merie was talking to the police, she suddenly noticed the kid, dragging his sled behind him, walking up to the hotel. She ran to him, tripping on the snow, and grabbing him hugged him tightly, tears running down her cheeks. After kissing him again and again, she asked, "Where have you been?"

"In Alexander Park," he answered.

"Don't ever, ever go to Alexander Park alone again!" She said.

Chapter Three:
Dinner At The Kremlin

One day, Rafal returned from work earlier than usual. "We have to get a babysitter for Alec this evening. We're invited together with the Communist Party leadership, the ambassador and the three secretaries, to a gala dinner with the Soviet top brass at the Kremlin," he said.

"Why didn't you tell me that a few days ago?" Merie asked.

"Because I was told about it just an hour ago. The dinner is in honor of the liberation of Warsaw by the Red Army."

"Will Stalin be there?"

"I have no idea. No one knows what his plans are. He just returned a few days ago from the Yalta Conference, where he met with Churchill and Roosevelt to discuss the coming situation in Europe. I think this dinner is being organized to update us. In one hour, a black limousine will take us to the Kremlin and bring us back at the end of the evening. We have to be properly dressed. I'll wear my official blue suit."

Merie asked their neighbors' daughter to watch over Alec. She then quickly bathed, dressed and put on her makeup, feeling at once both excited and anxious. She had never attended such an important event. The fact that they were invited was proof that the Russian leadership highly respected Rafal and his work.

As Merie and Rafal walked up to the black limousine that was waiting at the entrance of the Baltschug Hotel, the chauffeur, dressed in his uniform, stepped out and opened the car door for them. This was the first time Merie had ever been in a limousine. She smiled to herself – here she was, a nurse from an orphanage in Tashkent, going to dinner at the Kremlin.

"If we're going to celebrate the liberation of Warsaw and Poland, how about going to Pinsk and Horodno? I must find out what happened to my brother and my parents."

"Of course. We said we would do that. The colonel who helped us escape at the start of the war is now the commander of western White Russia. I'll ask him to help organize your trip as soon as possible."

As the limousine pulled into the Kremlin, the guards at the entrance asked for their names, and after being cleared they went on up to the entrance to the Politburo, the central seat of government.

The reception hall was glowing with bright lights from huge chandeliers, which were reflected in large mirrors, which covered the walls between the many windows. Merie took her place next to her friends from the embassy while Rafal went to greet his colleagues.

"Who can fill me in about the Russian side here?" she asked.

"That sour face over there in the corner who isn't talking to anyone," Olga whispered, "that's Vladislav Molotov, the foreign minister. Before you ask, that's the Molotov who divided Poland up. And that one over there with the white goatee, that's Nicolai Bulganin, deputy defense minister and Stalin's right hand in the military headquarters. And as for the one with the glasses and the scary look, you have to watch out for him. His name is Lavrenti Beria, head of the NKVD."

"And the big man standing next to him?"

"That's George Maximilianovich, member of the Politburo and very close to Stalin. In fact, he's the most senior of them all."

Just then, two marshals and their wives walked in.

"Who are they?" Merie asked.

"The tall one is Konstantin Rokossovsky, commander of the second Belarus front, and the shorter one is Georgy Zhukov, commander of the first Belarus front. I wonder why they were invited..."

General Zygmund Berling, commander of the Red Army's Polish Division, quickly turned to the two marshals, stood tall, saluted and shook their hands.

All the guests were then asked to proceed to the dining hall where a big oval table stood in its center. The chairs around it were upholstered in a deep, rich purple velvet and two huge chandeliers lit the expansive space. Malenkov invited everyone to take their seats. Next to Rafal sat Cyrankiewicz and next to Merie, Yaakov Berman, a member of the Politburo in charge of the security agencies in Poland. "Remember, I warned you not to start with the bread, even if they serve the freshest, most fragrant breads," Rafal whispered in Merie's ear. "The table will soon be loaded with many delicacies, so leave room for them."

"After three years in Tashkent, even if I don't touch the bread, I can't possibly eat all that food," Merie giggled.

"Hello, Rafal," Cyrankiewicz said. "Henryk Jabłoński from the Socialist sector of the Farmers' Party spoke very highly of you."

"Jabłoński?" Rafal was surprised. "We were a team, where is he now?"

"We brought him in to our government-in-the-making, and he's now in Lublin."

"Please tell him to get in touch with me through the embassy. I miss him and our talks."

An eight-course meal was served, accompanied by a seemingly unending supply of the finest wines. Towards the end of the meal, a side door opened and in entered a solidly built, short man with a pockmarked face, remainders of his childhood bout with smallpox. He sported a thick moustache and held a pipe between his lips. His army uniform was void of ranks, and only a golden star-shaped medallion was pinned to his chest, signifying him as "Hero of the Soviet Union." That was Stalin.

Everyone at the table stood up and burst into loud applause. Stalin raised his hands and thanked them with a slight nod. As everybody resumed their seats, Stalin raised his glass of vodka and invited everyone to do the same.

"I apologize that I was unable to join you earlier," he said. "The war that is now coming to an end, demands my full attention. But it is important to tell our Polish friends of the future of Poland, our esteemed neighbor. First, however, let us raise a toast to the liberation of Warsaw from the Germans! To a free Poland and to the Red Army that liberated her!"

Once again, Stalin bowed his head. "Comrades, several days ago, I attended the Yalta Conference where I met with Roosevelt and Churchill. I cannot divulge the decisions or agreements, which were reached, but the main and most important issue we discussed, was the future of Poland. Russia, which suffered the loss of millions of dead and wounded, has to shift its borders westward, in order to ascertain that never again will an aggressor try to invade that territory." Stalin took a sip from his drink, and the Politburo members exchanged tense looks as they waited for his next words. "At the Yalta Conference, the new borders of Europe were drawn. In the Balkans, Moldova was annexed to the Soviet Union. Romania, Bulgaria, and Yugoslavia, which will include Serbia, Croatia and Slovenia, will come under us."

Stalin looked intently at the audience and continued: "Hungary and Czechoslovakia will be under the auspices of the

Russian army. Eastern Poland will be annexed to the Soviet Union and Rovno and Lvov will be annexed to the Ukraine. Northern Poland will be annexed to White Russia. The Vilna region will be annexed to Lithuania. Lithuania, Latvia and Estonia will become republics within the Soviet Union. In return for Poland's loss of nearly fifty percent of its territory, eastern Prussia will become part of Poland, as will the area in western Poland up to the Nysa and Oder rivers. Polish citizens from east Lvov will be relocated to Poland, and the Germans will be sent west." Stalin looked directly at the Polish group and continued. "As I said, most of the discussions and disagreements focused on the Polish issue. Churchill," he said with disdain, "sees himself as the patron of the government-in-exile in London, and wants them to be appointed as the legitimate government, but that will not happen. The members of the government-in-exile, as well as the officers and soldiers of the Anders Army, will be able to return to Poland as Polish citizens, but not as an organized group. The only thing left for us to discuss is the matter of the free elections." Once again, Stalin paused and looked at his Polish guests. "I want Poland to be friends of the Soviet Union. I agreed to allow free elections in Poland and I expect you, the leaders of the Polish left wing, to win them which, I believe you will. And if not," he paused and studied the guests' faces, "if not, then we have the means that will see to it, such as the Red Army and the NKVD. Isn't that so, Comrade Beria?" Beria nodded.

"I apologize but I have to leave now," Stalin said. "I hope you have been provided with everything you need. Please, continue enjoying your meal," And he disappeared behind the heavy side door.

On their way back to the Baltschug Hotel, Merie sat in the back of the limousine, huddled in the corner, completely silent. She was incapable of uttering a single word.

Chapter Four:
A Visit To Horodno

In response to Rafal's request, General Vadim Alexievich Popov, also known as "the Colonel," sent Merie an invitation to come to his headquarters in Pinsk. "You promised, and you kept your promise," Merie said and hugged Rafal. "I'm so excited, and I'm so grateful that you've supported me on this, and are going to watch over Alec while I'm gone."

Rafal embraced her warmly. "I hope you get good news," he said and his eyes grew moist. "As you saw, you're scheduled to leave next Sunday. An officer by the name of Yuri Morozov will escort you, and from the moment you reach Pinsk, you'll be under the care of General Vadim Alexievich Popov's headquarters."

Rafal saw Merie to the West Moscow train station, where Captain Yuri Morozov, from the west Belarus Headquarters, was waiting for them. He saluted and said, "General Vadim Alexievich instructed me to escort Mrs. Gerber to his headquarters. I am glad to meet you." He then turned to Rafal and said, "Don't worry, comrade, we'll take good care of your wife."

"Yuri, you can call me Merie," she said.

The station's immense hall was swarming with Poles from eastern Poland, which has been annexed to the Soviet Union, as well as Polish Jews who had found shelter from the Germans in Russia, and were now returning to those areas liberated by the Russian army.

"Merie, I'm begging you," Rafal said as he embraced her, "don't do anything that can put you at risk. Listen to Yuri and follow his instructions."

Merie and the captain boarded the train which pulled out of the station, slowly gaining speed as it rushed forward. Merie sat near the window with Yuri facing her.

"The Rail Authority was forced to build detours due to the extensive damage to the rails and the train stations, so this trip may take two days."

Merie smiled. "Yuri, I didn't think this would be an easy journey. I have a great deal of experience riding trains in impossible conditions, for long distances."

The horrors of the war were reflected in the silent landscapes that rushed by as the train sped on. The earth is black, Merie thought sadly. Fires had burnt down houses that were once home to so many people, and families that no longer existed. She saw very few people from the train window. Millions of soldiers were killed, she thought as her eyes caught the trenches that had been dug to shelter the young lads who shed their blood, drenching the ground.

Late at night the train pulled into the Minsk station, where they waited for their connecting train to Brest that was to leave at dawn. From Brest, another train took them to Pinsk, where a military vehicle was waiting for them to take them to the Red Army headquarters.

Merie immediately went to General Popov's office. "You must be very tired and hungry," the General said when she walked in. "First, get some rest. There is a room ready for you where you can stay the night and tomorrow morning you will leave for Stolin and Horodno along with the Captain. I've ordered an additional escort of four soldiers and a sergeant because of the dangers along the way."

"Thank you, General. You were so kind to us in Rovno when we were forced to flee."

"Not to flee, to retreat," he said with a smile and stretched out in his armchair. "How is Rafal doing? Is he satiated with the Politburo and Stalin at the Kremlin?"

"Yes," Merie answered with a smile. "He is third secretary at the Polish Embassy in Moscow."

The General smiled. "You certainly didn't expect such a turnover when you sat with your infant son in your arms at the entrance to the Army's headquarters."

The following day, Merie and Yuri got into the HQ's official car with their entourage in the escorting jeep and they set out for Stolin. The deep imprints in the broken, rugged roads left by the heavy chains of the tanks that had battled here, and the burnt remains of homes, were silent testimonials to the war that had not spared Stolin.

The small convoy stopped in front of City Hall. Merie and Yuri went into the mayor's office. "We are here on behalf of the Military Governor of this region, General Vadim Alexievich Popov," Yuri began. "I ask that you answer the questions that Mrs. Gerber will ask you, as if the General was posing them." The mayor nodded.

Merie was highly agitated. "My name is Merie, my maiden name is Hackman," she said. "Was there a ghetto in Stolin?"

"Yes," the mayor replied.

"Were the Jews of Horodno sent there?"

"They were forcibly marched to the ghetto. Men, women, children, old people. As far as I know, there are no Jews left in Horodno."

"Did you know Mr. Hackman, who was a forestry advisor to the Polish prince?"

"I knew your parents. Mr. Hackman and his wife led the foot journey from Horodno."

Merie fell silent. "They had a son, he was very tall," she said with a shaky voice. "Was he also with them?"

"I don't recall a young man marching alongside Mr. and Mrs. Hackman."

"And what became of the ghetto?"

"The Germans and their Ukrainian helpers gathered all the Jews from all the surrounding towns and villages over a period of three months, and in September of 1942, they dug deep holes near the military airport. They marched all the Jews there and shot them. The Jews of Stolin and the surrounding area are all buried under three dirt mounds, as are your parents."

"Not one person survived?" Merie muttered.

"I'm sorry, Miss Hackman. I told you everything I know."

Merie glanced at Yuri. "Let's go," she said. "Captain, I'd like to go to Horodno. Maybe my brother is there."

The fifteen-mile ride to Horodno was familiar to Merie, yet now it all seemed strange. Everything was burnt black. The forest, which she used to frequent with her father, was filled with broken. The trees too took part in the war, she thought. Involuntarily, they protected the people who found shelter there hiding amongst their branches. Now both humans and trees are slaughtered.

The military vehicle stopped in front of the regional council building, from where Merie could see her parents' house in the distance, with smoke rising from its chimney.

She knew the council chairman and upon seeing him, she immediately said, "Stanislav, hello. I see smoke coming out of our home's chimney. Is someone living there?"

"Your neighbor, Vladimir, he took over the house when your parents were evacuated to Stolin," Stanislav replied. "There was nothing I could do to stop him."

"Bring him over here," Merie said. She sat silent and erect remembering Vladimir, the young lad who used to play with Gudel when they were children. A short while later, two soldiers entered the room, holding Vladimir by his arms.

"Do you recognize me, Vladimir?" Merie asked.

"Yes," Vladimir muttered. "You're Merie, Hackman's daughter. Gudel's sister."

"And you're living in our home."

"It... it stood empty... so..."

"And Gudel. You were close friends when you were children. Where is he?"

Vladimir's legs shook slightly. He opened his mouth to speak but nothing came out.

"Let me tell you about the events that happened," the council chairman said. "Gudel escaped to the forest and joined the partisans even before the Germans rounded up the Jews. Vladimir took over your family's house after the forced march to Stolin, but Gudel didn't know anything about the evacuation and came to the house to gather some food for him and his friends, and then he found Vladimir and his family living there."

"Where is he? Where is my brother?" Merie asked with tears rolling down her cheeks.

"He's gone, Merie. Vladimir handed him over to the Germans."

If only she could, Merie would have let out a loud wail of grief over the loss of her beloved brother whom she worshipped. "How... tell me how...," she murmured and couldn't stop the tears.

"I'm sorry to tell you that they hung him in the town square, with a sign around his neck: 'This is the end of every Jewish partisan.'"

"He was your friend, Vladimir, you were childhood friends!" Merie stood up and shouted at him.

Vladimir was silent, his chin was trembling and a pool of urine dripped between his legs. The council chairman nodded to remove him from the room. The room fell silent for a moment and then a shot was heard. Yuri returned to the room and said, "The prisoner tried to escape, we had no choice, we had to shoot."

"We will see to the traitor's burial," said the council chairman.

Chapter Five:
It's Over

At noon on the 8th of May 1945, the cannons lining the Moscow Riverbank along the Kremlin's wall thundered, announcing the end of the war. First, ten cannons thundered, which were followed by ten more, and then another ten. Merie rushed to the window. The cursed war was over. Berlin was conquered.

"It's over, it's over," she kept murmuring with tears in her eyes. On her bed lay the little outfit that her mother had knitted for Alec, the last thing that Gudel has given her. Never will she see him again. Never will he hold her hand again. Where has their childhood disappeared to, she thought. That time is gone forever. Who will remember Gudel and how gifted he was? Ever since learning of his death, Merie burst out crying uncontrollably again and again throughout the day.

Rafal returned to the hotel earlier than usual, carrying a bottle of wine. "We're going home!" He shouted. "We have to celebrate!"

"I wonder what you mean by going home. Which home are you referring to?"

"Everyone's going back to their homes and we're returning to Warsaw."

"To Warsaw that is under Stalin's rule?"

"To Warsaw that is under the rule of the Polish people."

"That's not what Stalin said at the dinner."

"That was nothing more than an announcement. We can return to Warsaw without any fear."

"I'm thrilled that the war is over, but I'm not going back to Warsaw and neither is Alec. I'll wait to see how things develop. Alec's not going to grow up in a country where his classmates will call him 'a dirty Jew,' in a land where his grandmother, grandfather and uncle were murdered. Do everything you can to see that your appointment here is extended, because I am definitely not going back to Warsaw with you."

"The ambassador doesn't want to lose me. I've been offered a position to set up the archives network in Poland and I might lose that opportunity if we don't go back."

"You won't lose a thing. It'll take at least two years until anyone can begin dealing with the archives."

"Merie, are we going to celebrate the end of the war or are we going to continue arguing if and when we return to Warsaw?"

Merie took the wine bottle from Rafal, placed it on the table and embraced him, holding him close for a long moment. She then went over to the cabinet and took out two glasses.

"A toast to peace!" Rafal said.

"I'll gladly toast to that," Merie said and clinked.

It was a cold wintry morning in June 28th. The skies were grey and rain fell intermittently. Everyone's eyes were glued to the great clock at the top of the tower in the Red Square. Ten loud-ringing cut the silence and two white horses dashed out from the gate of the Kremlin wall. On the first horse sat Marshal Georgy Zhukov, conqueror of Berlin, and on the second Marshal Konstantin Rokossovsky, commander of Operation Bagration and liberator of White Russia and Poland. They passed in front of one group of marchers after another, congratulated each one, who cheered with the Russian battle cry, "Hoorah, Hooraah, Hooraaah!" The Soviet anthem sounded while in the background the cannons thundered once again. There was a roll of drums and the military parade began. The division commanders marched in front of every square-shaped formation of rows of soldiers, each representing a different front. Behind them marched the Cossack cavalry, followed by the Soviet tanks and Russian and American vehicles. At the square, soldiers carried banners and flags of the major divisions of the Wehrmacht army. Merie and Rafal looked at the balcony where the Soviet Union leaders stood. A row of soldiers broke away from the square formation and threw down their flags at the balcony's base. They were followed by throwing down the flags of the German armies. Thus ended the military march of the German Wehrmacht's surrender to the Russian army.

Back in their hotel, Merie cooked a rich meat soup for her family, she felt happy. Suddenly a wave of nausea overcame her. She rushed to the kitchen, knelt down and began vomiting into a bucket.

"What happened?" Rafal, worried, rushed to her side.

"I think I'm pregnant," Merie said.

Chapter Six:
The Moscow Hotel

In October 1945, the Gerber family stood in the Moscow Hotel suite that had been allocated to them, and glanced around. It had just been vacated and they were promised it would be painted and cleaned before they moved in. As Merie looked about her, she couldn't stop smiling. There were two large rooms, one was a sitting room, and a master bedroom for them and for the soon-to-be-born baby, a fully equipped kitchen and a single room for Alec. Best of all, there was a small balcony.

"I think we're all set," she said to Rafal, who was leaning against the sitting-room wall. "There's also the large lobby downstairs where you can order coffee and sit with friends and diplomats. Perfect for you."

"You know that no one makes coffee like I do. Especially after I bought that little macchinetta from the Italian Politburo comrade. Making coffee is a serious matter," he added with a wink.

"Of course, but now let's get back to more serious matters. We need a kindergarten for Alec and a maternity ward for me, the baby is coming very soon."

"Embassy wives can give birth at the Clara Chetkin Clinic right across the main entrance to the Kremlin," Rafal smiled. "There, only the Communist Party and the military top brass are admitted, because it's the finest clinic throughout the Soviet Union. You'll have a private room and the very best doctors and midwives will look after you, and our child will always be able to brag that he was born in the Kremlin. If you agree, I'll see to it that you're given a preliminary appointment next week."

It was 1946, the coldest year ever.

Merie and Rafal held a party in their suite at the Moscow Hotel to celebrate the New Year. ,' Moscow was covered in a blanket of snow and Merie kept gaining weight. Every morning, special snow-clearing trucks cleared the streets, spreading salt.

On the night of February 21 a huge snowstorm blew into the city. Rafal was out at a meeting, and Merie asked him to return early as she felt the birth was near. At ten p.m., the first contractions began. Merie went over to the neighboring suite, where the embassy's first secretary resided, and knocked on the door. She had asked Sonia to watch Alec when the time came. . "Please look after Alec," Merie said the moment the door opened. "I feel I'm going to give birth very soon."

"Would you like us to order an ambulance to take you to the hospital?"

"I'll go down to the lobby and call Rafal. If he can't come, I'll call a cab," Merie said and rushed to the elevators. Rafal's office told her that he had just stepped out to a meeting, so she decided to take a cab. Every evening cabs were lined up at the hotel entrance for the guests, but that night the storm drove them away to their homes. Merie's contractions grew frequent and stronger, and she feared she would give birth there and then if she didn't reach the hospital soon. A cold wind hit her when she stepped out into the street. "It's one street, just seven hundred yards away," she whispered to herself. Heavy snow kept falling silently quickly covering the street with a thin white layer. She managed to take just a few steps and to grab a streetlamp. The next contraction was far stronger and she understood what that meant. The snow was getting thicker and deeper. I'll be okay, I'm making progress, she thought. I'm already a third of the way there. But once again a strong contraction came. I mustn't fall, if I fall I won't be able to get up, she thought. She waited until the contraction passed and trudged on. Chunks of ice stuck to her boots. What a mistake. Why didn't she call an ambulance? She mustn't slip, she mustn't fall, she kept thinking, when a contraction overwhelmed her and she lost her balance. 'I've hurt my child, I've killed my child,' she sobbed. With her last drop of strength, she managed to get up on her knees, grasped her belly when another contraction hit her, and screamed out in pain and fear.

Suddenly Gudel appeared in front of her. Not as she remembered him, but as they were as children. Tears ran down her cheeks while she imagined him gazing at her with his curious eyes, wondering, 'Where were you, Merie?'

The lights of a car suddenly flashed behind her and drew closer. The car slowed down and stopped at her side. The driver stepped out of the car into the stormy snow. "Anything wrong, Ma'am?"

"Everything!" Merie shouted out. "I'm in labor, I slipped and fell on my belly and I'm afraid I hurt my baby. Please, take me to the Clara Chetkin clinic."

"You're Merie? Come, lean on me and I'll help you into the car. We received a message from the embassy that a pregnant woman went out into the storm on her way to the clinic, so we were looking for you." Merie nodded. "I'm a doctor. Don't worry. Even if you fell on your belly, it doesn't necessarily mean you hurt the baby. Here, lean on me." He opened the car door. "Now slide along the back seat. We'll be at the hospital in two minutes. Everything will be ok."

They reached the emergency ward entrance. The doctor called the maternity nurses to help Merie out of the car and lay her down on a gurney that they rolled into the emergency room. For a moment, everyone fell silent as the doctor checked for the baby's heartbeat. "That's one of the strongest heartbeats I've heard in a long time," the doctor said. "We're about to have a new general, for sure."

Merie and Rafal's son was born the following afternoon at four o'clock. A maternity nurse carried the newborn infant to his father, and Rafal and Henryk Jabłoński gazed at him. Jabłoński asked to be the infant's godfather, and so the infant was given his name, Edward (Edjic) Henryk Gerber.

Chapter Seven:
A Signal From Warsaw

Merie was sitting in the lobby of the Moscow Hotel slowly sipping a cup of coffee. . She had just returned from a walk in the Red Square. The sunrays coming through the large hotel windows filled the lobby with a soothing ambiance. Edjic seven months old, was asleep in the baby carriage next to her. Suddenly, her friend Natan Rappaport entered the lobby waving to her with another man right behind him. Merie waved back and put a finger to her lips asking them to keep quiet.

"Hello, Merie. Congratulations on the birth of your second son. I'd like to introduce you to David. He just got in this morning from Warsaw and bears regards for you from Nahum Boneh."

"Nahum Boneh is in Warsaw? He's not in Kibbutz Shaar Golan?" she asked. "He was my counselor at the Movement's nest in Pinsk, and married my close friend, Pola, who studied with me at the *Tarbut* Gymnasia."

"Yes," David said. "Nahum was sent to Warsaw as the delegate of *Hashomer Hatzair* in Palestine. It's about his new job that I've come to talk to you. I asked Natan to introduce me to you."

"First, let me hand over my son to his nanny," Merie said and headed for the elevators with the baby. Ten minutes later, she returned. "Now we can talk," she said.

"Well, to put it briefly," David began, "Nahum reports directly to Meir Yeari, CEO of the Movement and leader of *Mapam*, the United Workers Party in *Eretz Yisrael, on* all that is happening in Poland. It took them some time to realize they need their own local representative. I was asked to help him, after I returned from Asia to Poland through the repatriation agreements with Russia. Nahum has a Palestinian passport, whereas I retained my original papers, so I'll be replacing him." Merie nodded, following his words closely. "We're aware that you and your husband helped several of the leaders of *Hashomer Hatzair* in Asia to reach Lublin, where they met with the partisans from Vilna, led by Abba Kovner, and set the Movement in Poland. But at the same time they set up the escape project from Poland to *Eretz Yisrael*." Merie moved uncomfortably in her seat. "We now have control of dozens of border crossings and a document forgery network."

"They set up *kibbutzim* in Poland?"

"Not only *kibbutzim*, but also youth movement nests and a counselor training network. Whoever escaped from Poland before the war or resided in Polish cultural zones, is allowed to return to Poland. It's important to build the system for the forthcoming repatriation. Setting up the communal *kibbutzim* was the most fitting way to train members of the movement for *aliyah*, immigrating to *Eretz Yisrael*. The movement focused on establishing these communal setups for the concentration camps survivors and those who returned from Russia. Abba Kovner left in 1945, going through Romania, but that route was quickly blocked. It was essential to stave off the exodus of leaders from Poland, because we believed that the post-war return of hundreds of thousands of Jews to Poland would leave them without a leader."

"I understand," Merie said, while she tried to figure out what was the point of that meeting.

"The local Poles were afraid of the great wave of returning Jews who would demand their property back and 'disinherit' the Poles, so to speak. Then the anti-Semitic right, that fought against the Communist government, sent murderers who got on trains and killed more than a thousand Jews."

Merie was shocked. "What action did the government take?"

"They tried to cope with it, but they failed. Then, on July 4 this year, an eight-year-old gentile boy ran away from home in Kielce and was found two days later. When asked where he had been, he said he was kidnapped and taken to the Jewish Community House, a building that accommodated families and individuals who had returned to their hometowns and found their homes had been taken over by strangers. This boy said there was another boy that the Jews had murdered and had used his blood to bake matzos for Passover. In short, a blood libel just like in the Middle Ages. At first, police and soldiers entered the building, but they didn't find anything to indicate or support this boy's story. What they did find were weapons for self-defense, and those were confiscated. Then the mobs assailed the building, brutally attacking the forty-two people who were living there. Men, women and children were murdered and many were wounded."

"But that's sheer anarchy if the police and army can't be relied on. How can anyone live in Poland like that?"

"This entire uproar happened while I was working on the Warsaw ghetto memorial monument, and the central figure in this monument is Mordechai Anielewicz, who was also in *Hashomer Hatzair* and led the Warsaw ghetto uprising," Natan continued. "Leaders of the Yevsektsiya, the Jewish section of the Polish Communist Party, opposed the coordination activities to retrieve Jewish children whose lives were saved during the war by hiding in monasteries and living with Polish families. They opposed the children's *kibbutzim*, which in my opinion is a great way to rehabilitate children who lost their parents in

172

the Holocaust. They also opposed the new nests established by the movement, and initiated a competing movement of Jewish Communists, and didn't allow us to appear in Jewish schools to recruit new members. In the end, they're also fighting the *Hashomer Hatzair* party. It seems that their only objective is to fight us. As if war is the one and only thing that defines them. So while the Yevsektsiya is doing everything in its power to minimize the *Hashomer Hatzair* and Anielewicz's role in the ghetto uprising, I believe that the ceremonial unveiling of the memorial monument will give our movement in Poland a push forward. Nahum Boneh needs help. After the events of July and August, he found himself in a crisis. Nearly all the old-timers are in Germany or in Palestine so he has to re-establish the entire network from scratch. That's why he sent me to meet with you."

"Why with me?"

"We spoke with the Asians who returned from Tashkent. They lavished praise on your actions and your contribution to the orphanage that was way beyond your duties. They said you're very strong and aren't cowered by authority. If you have a goal, you won't give up until you've achieved it. Besides all that, we heard you had dinner with the Soviet Politburo in person, and that you have connections with the Communist Party's Polish leadership. All this can help Nahum. He asked to tell you that he hopes you won't disappear on him like everyone else."

"I'm flattered by what you said," Merie smiled. "In so many words, I understand you're looking to end my comfortable life here in Moscow. I'll let you in on a secret. Rafal was offered an important position in Warsaw and he is eager to take it. But I told him I refuse to have my sons grow up in a country where 'Jew' is a curse. I can understand Nahum's needs and I really feel for him. However, the external circumstances and the internal problems practically turn his job into a mission impossible. But if he's sent a messenger like you to me, I will give his request some thought. I want to make clear that if I take any action on behalf of the Movement, it must be kept secret, even from my husband. And another thing. You will have to give me your word that if the borders are closed, you will see to it to bring my sons, my husband and myself to Palestine."

In the evening, as Merie and Rafal sat down to dinner, Merie said, "Maybe we should reconsider returning to Warsaw."

"Are you serious? You have always been strongly opposed to it."

"I want you to promise me that when I decide that it's time for us to leave, you won't stand in my way."

"I promise I won't stand in your way. My job here ends next March, so we can return to Warsaw in April, and I'll be appointed as secretary of the Jewish Historical Institute and a member of its Board of Directors."

"Is that what you want?"

"I was offered higher positions, but this position will suit me just fine. Merie, are you sure?" Rafal said and looked at her suspiciously. "What made you change your mind?"

Merie gave him a bright smile and kissed him. She knew that if she tried to explain, she would end up lying to him.

The following day, David returned to the Moscow Hotel for Merie's answer.

"Tell Nahum Boneh that next April we'll be returning to Warsaw. If he wants my help, I'll be able to do that."

4.

WARSAW 1947

Chapter One:
The Bristol Hotel

The Bristol Hotel, located on Krakowskie Przedmieście Street, was Rafal's family transitory link from Moscow to the Old City of Warsaw. Rafal had arrived in Warsaw a month before Merie and the boys and, in his search for a home for them, found a two-room suite at the Bristol Hotel.

In the lobby of the Moscow Hotel, Merie met with the women who had become her close companions in the last years, thanked them for their friendship and help and tearfully recalled that long-gone day when they had taken her to the department store where, for the first time, she saw such luxurious abundance.

The three boarded the train heading for Warsaw. Since the train was secured by Russian soldiers, Merie didn't feel anxious about the infamous murderous gangs that preyed on passengers. Still she was concerned that their return to Warsaw would prevent their immigration to *Eretz Yisrael?* What if she is the one who ultimately delaying that? The children were excited throughout the train ride, while Merie was a bundle of nerves.

At the Warsaw train station, Rafal was waiting for them. "How was the trip?" He asked as he hugged them. "Worse than ever," Merie replied irately. "The boys and I are exhausted."

The streets were dark and only the taxi's lights pierced the darkness and helped guide them.

"How did you find a suite in the great and affluent Bristol Hotel on Warsaw's most luxurious street?" Merie asked.

"If you've got the right connections, you don't need favors," Rafal chuckled. "We'll live there until our apartment is ready," he added. "We're close to the History Faculty at the university, where I'll be lecturing next year, and to the Jewish Historical Institute. And it isn't far from the school and the kindergarten, where I've already enrolled Alec and Edjic."

"So be it," Merie replied. "Let's just get there already. Tomorrow I'll find out what it is you're afraid to tell me."

The next morning, Merie looked out the window. "Rafal!" she called out. "Are we in Warsaw or is this a picture from Mars? Are you sure it's safe for us to live here? I won't be able to go out with the boys for a walk among all these ruins!" Warsaw was bustling with people and vehicles, but most of the houses in the nearby streets were demolished to some degree or another.

Rafal stood close to her, hugged her and looked out the window. "This isn't Mars. It's Warsaw. Actually, I was afraid you might not want to stay here. Our new home is being built in the Praga district, on the other side of the Vistula River, which sustained only slight damage. As soon as it's finished, we'll move. Besides, the Polish government is restoring the entire Stare Miasto area, the Old City, including our street. Come, Merie, let's sit down to eat."

While sipping his coffee, Rafal said, "I met a woman, her name's Marina. She'll be able to be Edjic's nanny and also see to the cooking and cleaning, leaving you free, as we agreed upon in Moscow. Also, I've been asked by the Culture Ministry to serve as advisor for the planning and construction projects. Perhaps that's another reason I decided to settle here, though I agree it's not a pretty sight. Let's later go see our new apartment and neighborhood."

Merie kissed Rafal's cheek and said, "I'm so proud of you. Even if it means waiting a few months until our home is ready, we'll manage. And about Marina, I'll be glad to meet her today, after we settle in. When can I go with you to the Jewish House? I want to look at the school and kindergarten."

"We can do that today," Rafal said.

"Tell me, the black phone in the entrance, is that for you?"

"Yes, but you're free to use it as you wish."

Rafal stepped out, leaving Merie in the expansive, pleasant suite. She went over to the phone, took out a slip of paper from her purse with the number David had given her in Moscow. "When you reach Warsaw, call," he said.

After several rings, a woman picked up.

"Nahum Boneh, please," Merie said in Hebrew.

"Who's asking?" The woman answered in Hebrew.

"Tell him Merie from Warsaw is calling. I'm at the Bristol Hotel, give him my phone number here please." Merie dictated the number.

An hour later, the phone rang and Merie rushed over to answer.

"Hello, Merie?"

"That's me," she said in Hebrew.

"This is Nahum Boneh. You speak Hebrew?"

"It's certainly not Polish or Yiddish," she joked.

"I'm glad you're back in Warsaw. David was very impressed with you. Right now I'm in Lodz, at the Movement's center."

"If the center is there, why did you want me to come to Warsaw?"

"We'll need you in Warsaw. When you go to the Central Jewish Committee, ask about the children's kibbutz at 38 Poznanska Street. It's run by Leibel Karieaski, from *Hashomer Hatzair* and the Zionist Coordination for reclaiming Jewish children. It takes care of orphans taken from Polish families and looks after repatriating them. . You can visit the place. That's it for now. When I return to Warsaw, I'll call you. I'm glad to have you aboard."

Merie replaced the receiver, and thought about what she had just heard. Everything sounded so clandestine. She decided that after she meets with Marina, she would contact Karieaski and set up a meeting with him.

Chapter Two:
The Children's Kibbutz

The Central Jewish Committee ran a school which taught in Polish. Merie preferred to have Alec attend a school more similar to that of *Tarbut* in Pinsk, but clearly, Rafal would find that problematic.

Rafal introduced Merie to the leading members of the Committee, which was mostly funded by the government. After the visit, she asked, "How is the children's kibbutz at 38 Poznanska Street connected to the Central Jewish Committee?"

"There isn't really a connection between us," one of the leaders replied. "There's a major war going on between the Zionist organizations and the Committee, which is subordinated to the Communist Party, over the fate of the orphans that during the war were placed with Christian families, and the repatriation children."

"It would be interesting to see what's being done there..."

As soon as Merie returned home, she called the kibbutz location and asked to speak to Karieaski.

"Hi. This is Merie Gerber speaking," she introduced herself. "I heard about you from Nahum Boneh and I'm interested in visiting your children's kibbutz."

"Nahum is a friend of ours. We'll be glad to meet you. What time tomorrow would you like to come?"

"I'll be there by ten a.m., the latest."

"Wonderful, I'll be waiting," he said and hung up. 'A very decisive type,' Merie thought to herself.

The next day, Merie knocked on the door of No. 38 Poznanska Street and a serious-looking six-year-old boy opened the door asking what she wanted. "I have an appointment with Mr. Karieaski," Merie answered in a serious tone.

"Sit down," the boy said, pointing to a chair in the hallway. "He'll be right here."

A few moments later, Karieaski arrived. "Hello, Merie, welcome to our children's kibbutz," he said, shaking her hand warmly. "Let's go to the office. I spoke with Nahum Boneh and I understand you're meeting with him next week. We'll be glad to host you here. But before I tell you about our kibbutz, tell me about yourself."

"I'm married and have two little boys. I'm a nurse. I worked at Czyste and during the war was the nurse at the Jewish Orphanage in Tashkent."

Karieaski smiled. "Circumstances have forced us to open a new type of orphanage. It all began when many Polish women turned to the Central Jewish Committee asking for financial support to look after the Jewish children they sheltered. We call these children 'the redeemed,' though it might not be proper to call them that, because some of them lived with very warm and caring families. We asked these women if they'd be willing to give these children up in return for compensation of between three thousand to five thousand zloty. For us it was very important to first bring these children back into the fold of the Jewish people, and then into the Zionist environment in the spirit of the pioneer youth movements. That's how the first children's kibbutz has started in Warsaw, and within a few months the idea caught on in Poland and dozens of such frameworks were established. Were you in *Hashomer Hatzair*?"

"Yes, and I studied at the *Tarbut* Gymnasia in Pinsk."

"Then it will be easy for you to understand our position. The children's *kibbutzim* are a combination of a youth movement's nest with a counselor who is also a teacher, and a cooperative educational structure. The older kids are waiting to make *aliyah* to Palestine. At first, we limited those who can join the kibbutz up to the age of twelve. The adolescents, thirteen years and older, were sent to *kibbutzim* for adults. But with the expansion of the Zionist Coordination for reclaiming children, which all the pioneer youth movements were part of, we had no choice but to open up the children's kibbutzim for children aged three to thirteen. Boys and girls reside in mixed quarters. They're responsible for preparing their own meals, cleaning and maintaining their rooms, and are learning the full meaning of a cooperative lifestyle in preparation for their *aliyah* to Palestine. Come, I'll show you around."

As they were walking through the courtyard of the orphanage, Karieaski pointed to the young boy who had opened the door for Merie. "You see the boy over there? He is the morning doorman, someone else in the afternoon will replace him. Come, let's go in," he said. "The first floor houses the movement's nest and the activity rooms, on the second floor are the classrooms and study centers, and the children's rooms are on the third floor, with four to six children in each room."

The children were in the classroom, studying arithmetic, while the younger ones were in the kindergarten playing. At the end of the tour, Merie said excitedly, "I'm so impressed by what you've done here and the methods you've adopted." Karieaski smiled. "How can I be of help to you?" Merie asked. "What is it that you need?"

"We need everything, and Boneh warned me not to pressure you, but if you want to help, I'll be thrilled if you could train our counselors."

"What do you mean?"

"Everyone wants to go to *Eretz Yisrael*. The adult members of the kibbutzim, who made *aliyah* and then returned to work in Germany in the returnees' camps, were our main counselors. Now we have to train new ones from among the younger repatriates. The 'nest' cannot operate without counselors. If you could meet with them even once a week, that will be a great help."

"In what areas do you want me to train them?"

"Whatever you choose. You can share with them your experiences from the orphanage in Tashkent, from your years with the Movement in Pinsk and the *Tarbut* Gymnasia, your work as a nurse, things such as first aid and even how to prevent epidemics. You can encourage them to share their experiences from the Soviet Union..."

Merie took a long moment to think things over. "I'll be glad to come on Monday from four to six p.m. and help in any way I can," she said. "I'll bring my older son with me, he's six."

Getting back, she said to her husband, "Rafal," "I visited the children's kibbutz on Poznanska Street today. I was so impressed by what they're doing that I promised to come on Mondays to help them..."

"You know, the Central Jewish Committee also runs orphanages," Rafal said.

"I know, but they also get help and financing from the Polish government and only twenty percent of the children are in their orphanages. Remind me again," she said sarcastically, "why are they fighting against the Coordination efforts and the pioneer youth movements?"

"You know, orphaned children need help even if they aren't Zionists."

"The children are guilty of nothing," Merie answered and sensed how her feelings of joy and optimism were slipping away. "It's the adults who are the criminals. The little help I can give I'll devote to the children's kibbutz."

Rafal remained silent. Merie noticed how his jaw muscles twitched each time he clenched his teeth. "By the way," he said, "Marina told me that when you weren't here, Nahum Boneh phoned. He said he'll call again tomorrow."

"What? Nahum? He was my counselor in Pinsk!" That was Merie's first lie about her secret activities. Even if there was some truth to it. But there, she had gotten through it all right.

Chapter Three:
Alma

I t was early morning when the phone rang.
"This is Nahum. Could you meet me today at twelve noon at 38 Poznanska?"

"I'll be there in an hour," Merie said.

"Marina," Merie called out, "I'm going into town in half an hour. Could you watch the children please?"

Marina's head peeked out from the children's room. "No problem," she said.

"Great," Merie replied and got ready to leave.

At the set hour, she rang the doorbell at 38 Poznanska Street. The serious-faced boy once again opened the door. "Mrs. Gerber," he said, "they're waiting for you in the director's office."

"Thank you. Would you be kind enough to show me the way?" Merie asked him.

Karieaski and two other men were waiting for her in the room. Nahum Boneh stood up and rushed over to Merie. "Finally! We meet," he said and embraced her, then he turned to the other man who was sipping tea. "I'd like you to meet Alexander," he said. The man was of average height and sported a thick, black moustache. He stood up, smiled, and shook her hand with a strong handshake. "I second Nahum's sentiments. Finally we all get to meet one another," he said. "I heard so much about you."

"Please, have a seat," Karieaski pulled up a chair for her. "I'll leave you," he said and left the room.

"It was important that you meet Alexander," Nahum said. "I move around between the 'nests,' the kibbutzim and the training programs, especially in Silesia, and now I've been recalled to *Eretz Yisrael*. The leadership has other plans for me. So it turns out there's no replacement at this point for my position and there's no one I can pass on the torch to, along with the many issues I was handling. Could you help Alexander until a new administrator arrives?"

"Alexander?" Merie asked. "I didn't get your last name."

"Alexander is enough," he said.

"I figure that's not your real name," she smiled. "Whatever. Are you from *Hashomer Hatzair*?"

Alexander smiled and glanced at Nahum. "You said she's quick. I am involved with the illegal immigration of Jews to Palestine. Officially, I'm the representative of the *Dror* Youth Movement, but in fact I'm here from the *Mossad LeAliyah Bet* that is secretly organizing the illegal immigration the British Mandate has forbidden."

"So, if I understand correctly, Nahum Boneh sent David to Moscow to ask me to return to Poland in order to help him, and before I've even had time to understand what he wants me to do, I'm handed over like some merchandise to Alexander from *Dror*, who doesn't even have a last name?"

"If you like, I'll give you three names to choose from. But more to the point, if you want to know, I live on a kibbutz, it's called Alonim."

"Okay, tell me more about your activities," Merie asked.

"As part of my job here in Poland on behalf of the illegal immigration efforts, I've been in contact with Russian officers who are in charge of various border crossings. During the escape, tens of thousands of Jews crossed into camps in Germany and Austria and since then are waiting for the decision of the United Nations' General Assembly on declaring a Jewish state. The elections in Poland this past January and the victory of the Communist Party, now called the United Workers Party, led to the closing of the borders. Those we were in contact with, disappeared into thin air or were replaced, and we are having a hard time understanding the current situation. I thought you could help us understand in which direction the wind is blowing, considering your husband's position in the Party."

"Are you asking me to risk the lives of my husband, my children and myself?"

"I'm not asking you to initiate any moves, just to pass on to me any information you might become privy to."

Merie asked to leave the office for a few moments. She wasn't sure how she could possibly play any role without endangering her life and the lives of Rafal and the boys. Does the end justify the means in taking such a risk? Could she herself serve as a rescuer of Jews?

Merie returned to the office. "Okay," she said, "I will help you."

"Thank you, Merie. Time is of the essence. You made the right choice in helping the children's kibbutz through training counselors. We can keep meeting here and passing information between us openly without needing to find excuses." Alexander said. "I suggest that, between your name will be Alma."

"Alma? You chose a pretty name for me," Merie said. "Tell me, is our meeting here connected in any way with the event to be held in Henryk Yabłoński's home? I know that Yaakov Berman, a Politburo member who is in charge of Poland's security agencies, will be attending. Are you aware of this event and are you expecting him to mention the matter we have discussed here?"

"Perhaps...," Alexander replied.

"Then why through me?" Merie asked. "After all, his brother, Adolph Berman, is one of the leaders of the Party in Poland."

"You're right," Alexander said. "There's just one problem. They're not in touch with each other. I'll give you a phone number Which you can use if you have any important message to pass on. Call from a public phone, say 'Alma' and hang up. Within a few hours, you'll get a call at home from the children's kibbutz, asking for your help with one of the children who felt sick. I will wait for you there."

Chapter Four:
A Meeting With Berman

The dinner at Henryk Jabłoński's home was held on May 2, following the celebrations of the First of May, and was attended by six couples of the leadership of the Communist Party and the United Workers Party. Merie wasn't surprised to see Yaakov Berman among the guests. Throughout dinner, he hardly spoke but closely studied all the others as they argued with one another. She noticed that every so often he would glance at her stealthily, and she wondered if that was because he liked what he saw or for other reasons. Lately, she had adopted a new habit of smoking. When the meal ended, she took a cigarette out of a well-crafted wooden box, placed on the table, and went to sit by the window, looking out at the ruined city "May I light your cigarette?" a voice sounded behind her and a hand holding a lighter appeared.

"Of course," she said. "Thank you, sir." She bent over the flame and lit up.

"I'm Yaakov Berman," he said. "And you are?"

"Merie Gerber," she answered, turning her face towards the window.

"Clearly, something is upsetting you, dear lady."

"My heart is broken looking out of the window," she replied.

"But as you can see," he said and drew closer, "every day more and more construction is going on, Warsaw is being rebuilt. Your husband has also been recruited towards that mission." Merie smiled.

"Merie" he continued, "let's cut the small talk. I have a message for the Movement contacts you're involved with, so please, listen carefully and remember what I'm about to tell you." He spoke so quietly that Merie had to strain her ears to hear him. Her heart was pounding and she felt tense. "The borders were closed, not in order to act against the Movement, but to prevent the escape of the Craiova Guardia's right-wing guerrilla fighters. We've decided to defy them. Either they accept our proposal for amnesty and integrate into the Polish society or bear the consequences."

"And what about the Jews who want to immigrate to Palestine?" She asked.

"A consulate or a legation will soon open here in Warsaw and then we'll renew the immigration process."

"What about the Yevsektsiya, they're aiming to damage the youth movements and the children's kibbutzim...," Merie asked.

"Forget about that, they're nothing more than dog fleas. All they can do is bite a little. Here too I have an important message. In a few days from now, the Soviet Union's UN delegate, Gromyko, is going to speak and he will announce that the Soviet Union will support the idea of establishing a national homeland for the Jewish people in *Eretz Yisrael*. Therefore, not only will the Soviet Union vote for the birth of the Jewish state, but all the other countries that are connected to the Soviet Union ideologically and politically, will do the same."

Merie finished smoking her cigarette and crushed the butt in the ashtray. "If you don't mind, I'll just go over to take another one," she said. She saw Rafal watching her, as she took another one and went back to sit in the same place.

"Merie, in his speech he will say that the Soviet Union supports the establishment of a bi-national state in *Eretz Yisrael*.

This, though, is nothing but lip service. Everyone knows war will erupt and, between us, Britain ignited this move, because it will be forced to leave the Middle East. The important message for you is that the Soviet Union will help in providing weapons from surplus stock, left over from the war, stored now in Czechoslovakia. A hundred and forty thousand people are waiting in the camps in Germany for the UN's announcement, approving the new Jewish state, to immigrate to *Eretz Yisrael*, and another several tens of thousands of Jews will be permitted to emigrate from Poland after that. That's how we will help our young state to win the war and establish itself."

Merie took a deep breath. "It doesn't sound like such a far-fetched scenario," she said, "but we'll have to cut this short. I must get back to the table."

"You're right. Please transfer this information to the proper people. Don't miss this opportunity."

"What were you talking with Berman about?" Rafal asked on their way home.

"About how a person experiences the destruction all around us. He promised that the government is doing all it can to rebuild Poland to its former glory. He even mentioned your contribution to that."

Rafal nodded his head with satisfaction, as Merie remained silent.

She was unable to fall asleep. She thought about the lies she was learning to tell, and consoled herself with the approaching opportunity to make *aliyah* to *Eretz Yisrael*.

The following morning she said to Rafal, "I haven't been out for a walk with my son for quite a while." She placed Edjic in his baby carriage and quickly walked over to a public phone. She deftly inserted the coins in the slot and dialed the number

Alexander had given her. "Alma," she said when the other side picked up, then she hung up.

An hour later, the phone in their apartment rang. "Yorek doesn't feel well. He's running a high fever," she heard a voice say. "Could you come and take a look at him?"

"I'll be there in an hour," she said, knowing she had to transfer Berman's message as quickly as possible.

Chapter Five:
16 Konopazka Street

Merie was helping Alec with his homework when Rafal walked in. "I have some good news for you," he said. "They finished building our house on Konopazka Street. We can start packing and get ready to move. We'll need new furniture, so I've already applied for a loan for thirty thousand zloty from the Historical Institute. You too are eligible for a similar loan and I think that will be enough to furnish our new home. Would you like to go see it?"

"This child will not be a Yiddish writer or artist," Merie said as she closed Alec's notebook. "Do you want to go see our new home, Alechico?"

"Yes!" Cried Alex in Polish.

"I'll be so glad not to have to look out at the ruins every morning and be reminded of what happened," Merie said as they got into a taxi.

The taxi drove over a wide bridge that connected the two sides of the Vistula River, and suddenly they found themselves in a different world: Streets that had remained intact, paved roads, undamaged sidewalks, and a lively flow of smooth-running traffic. In the past, the Praga district was Warsaw's stepchild, but now it had flourished into a city. When the taxi pulled up to 16 Konopazka Street, Rafal asked the driver to wait.

They climbed up the steps to the second floor and opened the door, which was not locked.

Merie wandered through the rooms, which still smelled of the newly applied whitewash. "I see there's central heating in the apartment," she said. "That's a great plus here in Warsaw's winters."

"Absolutely," said Rafal. "And by the end of the week, the apartment will be hooked up to the electricity and phone company."

"Who are the neighbors across from us?"

"Hirsch Samolar and his family. He's one of the leaders of the Yevsektsiya, or as they're popularly called, 'the Jewish Section of the Communist Party.' The eternal enemy that keeps harassing everything you're involved in."

"Like they say, out of the frying pan into the fire," Merie mumbled. "They don't have to know what I'm doing, so there'll be no cause for arguments. By the way, have you met his wife?"

Rafal snickered. "Hirsch is the better half of the Samolar couple. You'll be wise to keep your distance from her."

"And I thought that today you were bringing good news."

Merie didn't have to wait long before she met Mrs. Samolar. A short time after both families had settled into their new apartments, they got together at the Gerbers for afternoon tea.

At precisely five o'clock, there was a knock at the door. Hirsch was the first to enter, carrying a bouquet of flowers, with his wife right behind him. Merie and Rafal thanked them for the flowers and Merie invited them to sit down. Rafal went to the kitchen to make the coffee he was famous for.

"Where will your children attend school?" Merie asked, taking the initiative. When she looked at Mrs. Samolar's face, she knew she wouldn't be the first to initiate a conversation.

"I'm considering registering them at a Polish school," Mrs. Samolar answered.

"And what's wrong with a Jewish school?" Merie asked.

"You people from *Hashomer Hatzair* want students to study in Hebrew. Instead of teaching children to become responsible citizens in a people's democracy, you're teaching them Zionism. And whoever doesn't immigrate to Palestine or wants to remain in his own country and raise his children here, is not considered a good Jew!"

"Excuse me, madam; I don't recall ever talking to you before. How can know what my beliefs are?"

Mrs. Samolar moved in her chair uneasily. "But since you raised the subject," Merie continued, "I'll tell you that I believe that the Communist Party is working very hard at building and restoring Poland. The question is, why insist on living here and not in our homeland. Amazing, isn't it, that even Gromyko, in his speech before the UN General Assembly, expressed support for the establishment of a homeland for the Jewish people in *Eretz Yisrael*. I believe that's a very Zionist viewpoint, which is the common policy shared by the eastern European countries, including Poland. Yes, I'm a Zionist and I believe that *Hashomer Hatzair* is now carrying out sacred work here in Poland, after the war."

Mrs. Samolar shot up. "Hirsch," she said, "we've heard enough radical Zionist nonsense. I suggest we postpone our coffee drinking to another time." Hirsch stood up and the couple left.

"What happened? You managed to scare our guests away?" Rafal asked, holding the coffee grinder in his hand.

"You're late," Merie said with a smile. "She attacked me right from the start, I couldn't stay quiet."

"I knew no friendship would grow out of this," Rafal chuckled.

"Thank goodness the Friedmans also moved here," Merie said, "and that Yossi is Alec's age. It's amazing how quickly children get attached to each other and become best friends."

"I don't know if that was a smart move, to come head-on against Hirsch Samolar and his wife."

"Can they harm you in any way?" Merie asked.

"They might be a bother. We have no problem with Hirsch. His wife's the troublemaker. She's an overly ambitious woman who feels frustrated and angry that her husband got stuck with the Yevsektsiya, and she's even angrier that the wife of the Party secretary, Gamulka, who is a Jew, was appointed to categorize the Jews. Those who don't look Jewish and whose names should be changed are referred to the general Party, and those with a Jewish look are referred to the Yevsektsiya. Funniest thing is, that Gamulka's wife is the most Jewish-looking of them all, she's small and fat and with clearly Jewish facial features."

"How about us drinking that coffee you were about to make," Merie said.

"At your service, Ma'am," Rafal answered and turned to the kitchen.

The strong aroma of fresh coffee filled the air as they sat down in their living room. "Tomorrow I'm going to the children's kibbutz. I want to be there to hear the UN vote on establishing two states in *Eretz Yisrael*, for the Jews and the Arabs. If the UN approves the establishment of a Jewish state, it will be fantastic. We'll have our own land." As she spoke and sipped her coffee, Merie wondered if Rafal was aware that the announcement of a Jewish state would in fact be the first step separating them.

"You'll have both a state and a war," Rafal answered.

"True. If war is the price we'll have to pay for our self-determination and statehood, we will pay it."

"Everyone knows how to start a war, but not necessarily how to end it," Rafal said.

The children's kibbutz's dining room was bustling with the kibbutz children and the adults from the *Hashomer Hatzair* and *Dror* youth movements. A radio was placed in the center of the room which despite the freezing weather, was warm with the presence of so many, whose full attention was now directed to the voice of the Brazilian chairman of the General Assembly. He called out each member nation and then repeated their vote. The tense silence throughout the dining room was tangible. The 'Pro' votes were increasing. Merie waited anxiously to hear the Soviet Union's vote as that of the Ukraine and Belarus, the eastern European countries and Poland. For a moment, she feared that perhaps Berman's message was mistaken. The Chairman announced the final count: Thirty-three 'Pro,' thirteen 'Con,' ten abstentions.

Loud exited cheers burst in the room. "We have a Jewish state!" Everybody hugged one another and then they all linked their and burst into a wild *hora*, the pioneers' traditional dance. Merie was swept into the enthusiastic dancing. Suddenly, she caught sight of Alexander who was watching her. She pulled away from the circle and went up to him.

"He kept his word!" She shouted, her eyes sparkling, as they embraced.

"You know," Alexander said, "we passed the message you delivered to us on to our leadership in *Eretz Yisrael*. You have no idea how much you helped us."

Chapter Six:
Rebecca

The roads were covered with snow and with high piles that the municipal workers cleared from the streets every morning. Merie went out to bring Edjic home from the Jewish nursery school he was attending. The gate was locked so she rang the bell and the teacher came out to let her in.

"Why was the gate locked?" Merie asked.

"It looks as if the anti-Semites are busy, despite the police attempts to keep the peace calm," the teacher said. "The children are going to leave in about ten minutes and a police car will be standing outside."

Edjic, who was almost two years old, ran up to his mother, who bent down to hug and kiss him. "Put your coat and scarf, on" she said, "it's very cold outside." As the little boy rushed to pick up his coat, Merie suddenly spotted Alexander helping a little girl put hers on.

"Alexander, you keep showing up in the most unexpected places. I understand you're Miri's father," she smiled at the child. "Miri, you and Edjic are best friends, aren't you?" The little girl nodded bashfully and buried her face in her father's legs.

"My dear Merie, this is the first time I'm here to pick up my daughter. My wife and daughter can join me now going to *Eretz Yisrael*. But since the situation is still somewhat unsettled, they'll be moving to Prague."

"And what about you?"

"I'll stay here and visit them every two or three weeks. It's closer than Palestine."

"So this is where Alma takes her leave of you?" she whispered.

"No, no... Nothing's changed, and as we talking," he came up closer, "will there be a meeting of the leadership to designate the New Year?"

"It seems you know better than me where I'll be spending this evening." Alexander smiled under his black moustache.

"Let's go, Edjic. Say goodbye to Miri's father," she said. Edjic raised his little hand and waved to Alexander.

Merie rushed home. She had to get ready for the New Year's dinner. Rafal was already at home and Marina took over the care of the children.

"I had a meeting with the head of the History Department at the university," Rafal said.

"Fill me in on the way. Did you order a taxi?"

A taxi was waiting for them downstairs. "How was your meeting with the head of the History Department?" Merie asked as soon as they were seated in the back of the taxi.

"It was good. They've hired Henryk Jabłoński. I might join the department next year."

"Is that what you want?"

"I always dreamed of being part of the teaching staff one day at the department where I studied."

I wonder what he'll be willing to give up, Merie thought, and in her heart the pendulum began swinging to one side.

At the dinner, the Party secretary and his deputy both welcomed in the New Year. They forewarned against a possible confrontation with the western European countries and the United States, and then asked everyone to raise their glass and toast the new and successful New Year. Rafal in conversation with his friends so Merie began to wander around the large hall. She stood by the window and took out the single cigarette she had with her. When she looked for a light, a bluish-yellow lighter flame touched her cigarette. Yaakov Berman again.

"You always surprise me," she said.

"Was the information I gave you about the Russian support and our bloc's support of a Jewish state, correct?"

"Couldn't be more so," Merie answered and smiled. Berman smiled back.

"And what about weapons?"

"Weapons will be provided. Czechoslovakia will see to that. You can pass that information on to your comrades." And he vanished away.

Her eyes met Rafal's. Was he suspicious? She came up to him and leaning over him, whispering in his ear, "I'm going home. Edjic wasn't feeling well earlier today.." Rafal kissed her on her cheek and nodded.

Getting her coat, she stepped out into the cold night air. A taxi was standing at the curb, waiting for the guests. She gave the driver her address and the taxi started out on its way. As they approached the Bristol Hotel, Merie asked the driver to let her off and wait. She hurried into the hotel lobby and went over to the public phone booth, and dialed the number Alexander had given her. After three rings, the receiver on the other end was picked up. "Alma," she said and hung up.

When she reached the apartment, Marina immediately told her there was an urgent call from the children's kibbutz. "They told me to tell you that Rebecca's fever has gone up."

"Thank you, Marina," Merie said. The day before, Rebecca had sustained a deep scratch from a rusty pipe so Merie was not sure whether the message was the agreed upon code or a genuine emergency.

Calling the kibbutz the head counselor told her, "Rebecca's in a bad state," "Besides a high fever and pain, her leg is giving off a bad smell. I didn't want to disturb you, but I know how much you love this girl."

"I must go to the kibbutz immediately," Merie said to Marina. "If anyone calls and asks for me, say I'm on my way to the kibbutz. When Rafal returns, tells him I went out on an emergency to the kibbutz."

Chapter Seven:
Scyste

Rebecca was in bed, burning with fever. "Let's take a look at your leg," Merie said stroking her cheek. The girl was shivering as Merie unveiled the bandages off her leg. The smell of rot hit her. "You must call an ambulance and bring her to Scyste Hospital immediately," Merie told the head counselor and turned to leave the room. "Merie," the guard standing outside the door called to her, "there's someone waiting for you in the director's office."

Alexander was sitting in the office. "How did you manage to put together such a quick cover?" He asked.

"It just so happens that there is a real emergency here, so let me just quickly tell you that Czechoslovakia is planning to supply weapons and ammunition to *Eretz Yisrael*," she told him as the sirens of an approaching ambulance grew stronger and stronger.

"That's an extremely important message!" Alexander said. "We're in touch with the Czechs, but we didn't know it's the eastern bloc's strategic decision."

"Please pass the message on. I apologize, I must escort a little girl to the hospital. Bye, Alexander."

Two orderlies moved Rebecca to a stretcher. "The Scyste emergency room," Merie instructed them.

"You mean Municipal Hospital No.1?"[2]

"Yes. The hospital in Scyste. I'll ride with you."

---

2   *Up to World War II, the hospital was called "The New Orthodox Jewish Hospital," and after the war, it was rebuilt and called "Municipal Hospital No.1." Today it's Szpital Wolski.*

Merie filled in the nurse in the emergency room with the necessary details, "Her name is Rebecca. She was injured by a rusty iron pipe, a deep infection has set in and she's running a high fever."

"Let's transfer her to the bed," the nurse said. "We'll do the intake and continue from there."

The nurse cleaned the wound, but there still was a black strip around it, which meant gangrene had set in. Rebecca screamed in pain and didn't stop crying. She held tightly onto Merie's hand while Merie stroked her hair and tried to calm her as the nurse changed the bandages.

"We'll give her medicine to take down the fever so she can sleep," the nurse said.

"In which ward will she be placed?" Merie asked.

"I assume she'll be transferred to the infections ward or the orthopedic surgery ward, it's run by Professor Lieberman, Alfred Lieberman," the nurse replied.

"Excellent. Please tell him I'll be back here in the morning and wish to talk to him before any decision is made."

The nurse noted the details on the intake sheet and attached it to the metal clipboard hanging from the bed.

"I'll pass on your message to Professor Lieberman," she said.

Merie bent over Rebecca and placed a kiss on her forehead, which was burning with fever. "I'll be back soon, dear, I'll come in the morning," she whispered.

In the taxi, on her way home, all the dramatic events of the day whirled in her mind in a jumble: The toast for the new year at the United Workers Party center; her talk with Berman that once again surprised her; her meeting with Alexander. What caused him to recruit her and turn her into Alma? She smiled to herself. She? A spy for the illegal immigration alliance? How amusing.

Chapter Eight:
Professor Lieberman

Professor Lieberman entered his office, together with two department heads and two interns wearing their blue surgical scrubs. "There is a lady waiting to see you, Professor," his secretary said.

"I told you I have no time for visitors," Prof. Lieberman snapped, but just then Merie walked in and his jaw dropped. "Merie?" he cried and spread out his arms to hug her.

"I haven't seen you in ten years," he said. He turned to the interns. "Tell the operation rooms to postpone the operations by half an hour." The doctors exchanged surprised looks with his secretary and left the room.

"How about something to drink? Coffee? Tea?" He asked and sat down.

"I'll have coffee if you'll join me."

"Tell me, where were you during the war?" he asked. "I wondered what happened to you and I'm glad to see you're blooming." Merie looked at him and told him the many hardships she had been through.

"In that case, we both went though much the same," he said. "I was recruited before the war as a physician in the Seventh Cavalry Brigade. During the war, we retreated along with the rest of the army towards the Romanian border, where we were taken prisoners by the Red Army that came from the east." The professor halted for a moment. "After the brigade was disbanded, I stayed back in Lvov as a doctor. Like you, I escaped to the east and in the end reached Tashkent, where I worked in a Russian hospital. When the Anders Army began taking shape, I tried to join them but was rejected, probably because I'm a

Jew. When the war ended, I returned to Warsaw with the repatriation agreement and then continued here to Scyste, where I've been the department director for the past three months. That's the long and short of it. Now it's your turn. Tell me, what brings you here?"

"Yesterday I brought in a young girl, her name is Rebecca."

"Rebecca? I was about amputate her leg. We examined her this morning and saw that the infection is spreading quickly and if we don't amputate, she may die. The earlier we do it, the better."

"Professor Lieberman, I'm begging you, please put off the surgery for several days. Many cases of infection of the limbs ended up with amputation, but many others were treated with the Kali baths and we succeeded in saving the children. Kali in high concentration is highly oxygenated and can be used to treat severe infections. Rebecca is an orphan, Professor Lieberman, she has no family. She is supposed to make *aliyah* to Israel this year with the Youth Aliyah program. If she loses a leg, what will she do? She will be transferred to a Polish orphanage and will waste away there."

"That's all very interesting, but the infection is spreading. Perhaps if we first drain the infection and clean the blackened flesh, we will then be able to treat her wound with Kali baths. Look, Merie, the child has to be bathed at least three times a day, for an hour each time. But we don't have the manpower to see to that."

"I'm ready to do it."

"Okay, great" the professor said. "Today, we'll do the drainage and tomorrow we'll start with the treatment for one week. But if the infection becomes worse, even slightly, we will amputate immediately."

"Agreed," Merie said. "Give me a week and then we'll see."

"You're the same stubborn Merie you always were," Professor Lieberman smiled. "Too bad there aren't more stubborn nurses like you. I hope we won't regret this."

Merie walked around the desk and gave him a hug, and kissed his cheek. "Great," he laughed, "if postponing surgery earns me a hug and a kiss from you, I think I'll stop operating."

Merie rushed to Rebecca's bedside. She found her cheeks in tears. "They want to cut my leg off," she cried bitterly. "How will I march at the dedication ceremony of the monument? How will I make *aliyah*?"

"No need to worry. At this stage, all they're going to do is clean your wound. You have to eat your meals and help me help you. That's the only way we'll be able to fight the infection."

"I promise I'll do anything you ask, just don't let them cut off my leg. Who will want a girl with one leg?"

"You, Rebecca, will always be wanted, whether with one leg or with two. Come, let's remove the bandages and see how you are doing. A nurse will soon be here to take you to the surgery department."

Chapter Nine:
The Procession

Two weeks after Rebecca was admitted to the hospital, a pinkish strip of healthy tissue appeared on her leg. Professor Lieberman entered her Room trailed by interns and students. A bowl filled with the dark purple Kali liquid stood beside her bed. Merie had just finished her treatment.

"Good morning, Rebecca. Let's see how your leg is doing," Professor Lieberman said. Merie removed the bandage from Rebecca's scrawny leg.

"Should we postpone the amputation by another two weeks and continue this experiment?" The professor asked.

"I think we should, Professor," an intern said.

"I agree. We will wait two more weeks and then either we will release Rebecca for continued treatment at the orphanage or, if the situation turns, we will operate." The professor wrote down his conclusion on the patient's log clipped to the bed, and the group of doctors and students left the room.

"I promise you I will do everything I can to prevent your operation," Merie said. Tears rolled down Rebecca's cheeks. "In a month from now, the monument's dedication ceremony will be held and you will march with us in the procession."

"I love you so much," Rebecca said.

"And I love you too," Merie answered, wiping away a tear. "Tomorrow I won't be able to come, but a nurse will be here to look after you. And the day after tomorrow, we'll be back on schedule."

Merie entered Prof. Lieberman's office. "So what do you say about her progress?" She asked with a smile of victory. "Have you seen her progress?"

"You... Merie, your determination conquers every infection. Every obstacle."

"Professor Lieberman, tomorrow we are hosting Natan Rappaport in honor of his memorial monument to the ghetto uprising. You and your wife are invited to join us for dinner."

"We'll be more than glad to come."

Merie has hosted less frequently after the family had moved into their new home. The first to arrive were Natan and Sonia. Rappaport, who had just returned from Paris, and brought a bottle of select French wine. Then Professor Gishtur and his wife arrived. He was Rafal's close friend, and the head of the History Department at Warsaw University. He was a tall man with a serious face and, oddly enough, his wife looked very much like him. Professor Henryk Jabłoński and his wife soon came as well. Although Professor Jabłoński was a member of the Polish Socialist Party, ever since the Communist Party and the Workers Union Party had merged, he has gained a higher political status. The last to arrive were Professor Lieberman and his wife, Martha. The guests took their seats around the dinner table.

"Where are Alec and Edjic?" Natan asked.

"They're sleeping," Merie said.

"I brought gifts for them. I wanted to be there when they open them."

"Thank you, Natan. They'll be happy to open the gifts tomorrow," Merie smiled.

"Let me help you serve," Martha offered, with Sonia right behind her.

"No need. Please, relax. Marina will serve the meal."

Rafal opened the bottle of French wine. "Dear friends," he announced, "we have here two bottles of very fine wine. One, a dry red from France and the other, a semi-dry white from Hungary."

After filling everyone's glasses, he raised his. "Natan," he said, "we are about to dedicate your fantastic monument in memory of the Warsaw uprising. The support and excitement over your creation cuts across all sectors, from the Jewish Committee, the Zionist youth movements and even the Polish government. It is our great honor to have you here as our guest tonight."

The guests raised their glasses in a toast. "As we're celebrating," Professor Jabłoński said as he stood up, "Here's another reason to celebrate. Yesterday I was invited to a meeting with our Prime Minister, Cyrankiewicz. Rafal, I think you met him at the dinner with the Politburo, when Stalin shared his plans for Poland." Rafal nodded. "Well, Cyrankiewicz is planning to offer you the position of executive director of Poland's archives, directly under him. According to him, this position is extremely important nationally."

"But it was agreed that Rafal will join the History Department next year," Gishtur said.

"Correct, but that will have to wait until he finishes setting up Poland's new archival network," Jabłoński replied.

"Tell me, what other surprises are you going to pull out of your hat tonight?" Rafal chuckled. "You forgot that we're gathered here in honor of Natan?"

"I'm through," Jabłoński said.

"Me too," Gishtur smiled.

"And what about you, Professor Lieberman, are you also planning to offer me a position?"

"Lucky for you, we have nothing planned for you. But Merie is doing an outstanding job in our department and everyone has nothing but praise for her. She hospitalized a young girl who suffered from a terrible infection in her leg, and we were about to amputate to save her life, but Merie asked that we give her some time to try to save the leg with baths of Kali. The treatments worked and we are planning to publish a research paper on this case and its treatment protocol in the Polish Orthopedics Journal."

"Okay, dear friends," Merie said. "Enough talking about us. Natan, do you have any idea what *Hashomer Hatzair* is planning for the dedication ceremony?"

"I know there will be a ceremony attended by government officials and the Jewish Committee. Speeches by VIPs," Natan said.

"That's right, there will be speeches by VIPs. For us in *Hashomer Hatzair* and the other Zionist movements, what's important is the procession that will precede the ceremony. We will bring thousands of the Movement's members to Warsaw and we will all be wearing the Movement's uniform. There will even have representatives coming from *Eretz Yisrael*, with intellectuals and political leaders. The memorial monument represents the heroism of the Ghetto fighters, who were led by members of *Hashomer Hatzair* and *Dror*, and by the leader of the uprising, Mordechai Anielewicz."

"Communists and members of the Bund were also among them," Rafal added.

"Yes," Merie said, "but we won't open that discussion now. We've invited our friends here to celebrate together." She rang a small bell telling Marina to bring in the next course.

Jabłoński chortled. "Merie, tell me, in the communes in *Eretz Yisrael*, where your friends live, do they also ring a bell to have their food served to them?"

"No, Henryk. In the kibbutzim in Israel, the members get their own food. As a progressive socialist, you should be aware of that and appreciate it."

"Stop teasing each other," Rafal said. "I suggest we raise another toast to Natan and the memorial monument."

That was his third glass. He couldn't tell if the dizziness that he felt was the result of the wine or of the news he had heard about his future.

On April 19, 1948, the monument in memory of the Warsaw ghetto uprising was unveiled. It was placed in the square from which the Jews of Warsaw had been transported to the death camps. Twelve thousand people marched in the procession that preceded the ceremony. An immense number of marchers wandered amongst the ghetto ruins, between the buildings that had once been filled with the last soft voices of infants. Not a single house in the ghetto remained standing.

The procession was led by the heads of the Jewish congregation, together with Polish ministers and leaders, and intellectuals and leaders from *Eretz Yisrael*, including a renowned writer, military commanders and the future first ambassador of the State of Israel to Poland. A delegation of more than a thousand marchers represented the Polish *Hashomer Hatzair*, led by a young boy and girl who proudly carried a wreath shaped in the movement's emblem. Amongst the marchers were members of the children's kibbutz in Warsaw and with them a girl who limped slightly. Rebecca was marching hand in hand with Merie.

Chapter Ten:
War In Eretz Yisrael

The preparations for the procession and ceremonial unveiling of the monument diverted the attention from the unfolding events in Israel. From the moment the UN decision was declared, war broke out between the Israelis and the Palestinians over the main access roads and highways. Merie learned of this from bits and pieces of information while at the children's kibbutz.

Hearing that one day after the British mandate in Palestine had ended, the armies of seven Arab countries attacked Israel, she knew that the battles there were intense. She hadn't heard anything from her friends in Kibbutz Shaar HaGolan and was very anxious and worried.

On Tuesday, when she came to the children's kibbutz to treat the children's wounds and illnesses, Alexander was waiting for her at her desk in the infirmary. They hugged and she said, "It's been quite a while since I last saw you!"

"My family and I are spending most of our time in Czechoslovakia. Actually, the nature of my work has changed from what it was during the war. On the one hand, there is no longer the issue of certificates, everyone in the camps can make *Aliyah*, on the other, will there be a country left to immigrate to at the rate the battles that are now raging there?"

Merie covered her mouth anxiously. "So what do we do?"

"A lot," Alexander answered in a whisper. "Up to early June the Israelis managed to hold their own with the forces they had. They relied mainly on the kibbutzim along the borders as a frontline defense. Then the UN declared a ceasefire, and ever since the temporary truce, we've been bringing tens of thousands of youngsters to Israel from the camps in Cyprus, Italy, Austria and Germany. Our goal is to bring to Israel as soon as possible sixty thousand young men and women, equip them with weapons, train them and, in fact, build Israel's defense forces."

"Where will the weapons come from?"

"That's why I'm here to thank you. Your report from your meeting with Berman earlier this year confirmed other information we had, regarding the Soviet loc's support of Israel. You then mentioned Czechoslovakia and indeed, our people in the United States succeeded in purchasing several large cargo planes, they recruited teams of Jewish soldiers and flew them to Czechoslovakia. For a month now there's been an air bridge from there to Israel. We called it "Operation Balak." We even had our first pilot training course in Czechoslovakia. When the temporary truce ends, the Arab forces will be facing a totally different army."

"I'm glad," Merie said. "Did you happen to hear anything from Nahum about my friends in Shaar HaGolan?"

"Yes. The kibbutz was overtaken, looted and destroyed, but most of its members survived."

Once again, Merie covered her face. "Tell me. Tell me, Alexander, what happened in the kibbutz."

"The Syrians invaded the Jordan Valley and took over the town of Semakh, a border town between Syria and Israel. Our defense line was based on the kibbutzim Degania Aleph and Degania Bet, Beit Zera, Afikim and Ashdot Yaakov. Shaar HaGolan and Masada are two kibbutzim that extended eastward beyond this defense line. Syrian forces attacked them from the east. When the kibbutz members realized no supporting forces would be sent to help them, they decided to retreat to the major defense line, about a mile and a half to the west. The Shaar HaGolan people retreated to Beit Zera and the Masada people retreated to Afikim." Alexander paused for a moment. "The Syrian forces entered the kibbutzim and robbed them, then destroyed and set fire to most of the buildings. At the same time, they also attacked Degania Aleph and Degania Bet. After a long and bloody battle, the Syrians finally retreated from Semakh, Shaar HaGolan and Masada. The kibbutz members then returned to what was left of their home and began the work of rehabilitation."

"Do you know what happened to Nahum and Pola Boneh and the others from Pinsk?" Merie asked.

"I don't know about the other Pinsk people, but I know that Nahum and Pola are fine and well. He sends you his regards and asked to tell you that soon a new delegate of the *Hashomer Hatzair* leadership will be arriving, and he'll contact you then."

"And who's the new 'talent' they're sending us?"

"He really is a talent. His name is Moshe Tsizik, but he goes by the nickname Califf. He's in a different league altogether. He's not answerable to anyone."

"Oh, I know him from the movement's nest in Warsaw from before the war. It's about time they sent a decent leader who will put an end to all the mess here."

"What do you mean?" Alexander asked.

"*Hashomer Hatzair* in Poland was established by a group of amazing, wonderful people and included veteran movement members from Asia, partisans who came from the forests. They took it upon themselves to organize the escape network and at the same time initiated an exceptional youth movement, as well as a political party that even ran in the elections for the Polish parliament."

"So what's the problem?"

"They're burned out," Merie said. "They're endlessly arguing about how to unite the left-wing parties, and other petty political battles. A war is going on in Israel for its very existence, so many young people are being killed, a new state is being born and they're busy arguing what percentage each sector will get in running the party, which may not even exist a month from now."

"The left-wing parties in Israel united together to form a Labor Party."

"But in Israel, they put an end to the arguments a while ago. Here they're still fighting with each other as if Poland is the Promised Land," Merie said.

"So what do you suggest?"

"The youngsters under the leadership of Mishka Levin and Matityahu Mintz are for focusing on the youth movement and educational issues. They must make *aliyah* to Israel as soon as possible and find a way to encourage young activists to take leadership positions. The problem is that Israel's representative here doesn't have the authority or the power to finalize things. If the direction is *aliyah*, why bother maintaining the political parties? Why aren't the resources invested in the youth movement in order to prepare them for their move to Israel?"

"You sound like a political activist," Alexander said with a smile.

"If we send away all the young counselors, who will hold the movement together?" Merie asked. "Who will be responsible for the youngsters? Tens of thousands of young boys and girls are waiting in the displaced persons camps to make *ali-yah*. That's where the recruiting efforts must be focused! Okay, enough said," Merie waved her hand dismissively. "And you, keep me away from politics. In just a few months from now, Rafal will be appointed director of Poland's archives, directly under Prime Minister Cyrankiewicz. This isn't the right time for me to cultivate political Zionist activity behind his back."

Chapter Eleven:
Califf

A cold wind was blowing. Winter was drawing near, Merie thought as she entered the infirmary at the children's kibbutz. Alexander and Califf were waiting for her there.

"Hello Alexander, hello Califf," she shook hands with them. "Please, take off your coats and have a seat. Would you like something to drink?"

"Coffee will be nice," Califf said.

Merie stepped out and asked Pesya, the children's counselor, to prepare a pot of coffee.

"Entertaining young men, are you?" Pesya asked.

"Very young..." Merie chuckled.

"I'll bring in the coffee in a few minutes," Pesya said, "go back to your guests."

"Okay," Merie said. "What brings you here on this wintery day?"

"I came to say goodbye and to introduce Califf to you," Alexander said. "He is the representative of the head leadership in Poland and was sent here to revitalize the *Hashomer Hatzair* movement."

"I'll take it from here," Califf offered. "Look, I asked to meet with you as soon as possible, first because I heard a lot about you back home in *Eretz Yisrael* and your contribution to the Zionist Coordination Committee for the Redemption of Jewish Children, here at the children's kibbutz. I arrived in Poland two weeks ago and I have carried out a preliminary survey on the Movement's activities in Poland."

"And what conclusions have you reached?"

"Well, I'm of the opinion that the political party of *Hashomer Hatzair* is disintegrating. The party leaders are busy arguing about the structure of the union between the left-wing Zionist parties. If you ask me, since all that's left in Poland is the Workers Union Party, which is a Communist party, the day will soon come when no Zionist parties will be left in Poland."

"I agree with you," Merie said. "Rafal is one of the leaders of the Yevsektsiya, the Jewish section of the Communist Party, and they are setting up a Jewish scout movement to attract Jewish youth away from the Zionist youth movements, first and foremost, from *Hashomer Hatzair*. They're not at all fond of the Zionist parties in Poland."

Califf nodded in agreement. "I would like to focus on the educational movement whose banner is *aliyah*, immigrating to Israel. Whoever joins us will be brought to Israel, along with their families. I believe that the Jewish population in Poland is divided into two groups: The healthy, Zionist section that wishes to make *aliyah*, and the weak section that chooses to stay in Poland."

"As far as I know, the movement's leadership in Israel, along with the leaders of *Hashomer Hatzair* in Poland, don't share your clear-cut outlook."

"Then what do you think?" Merie said.

"Like you, I think that this whole business around the Zionist and non-Zionist parties will come to an end within a year or two."

"That's why we need to focus on *Hashomer Hatzair*, to help the movement grow as much as possible, and train its members towards making *aliyah*. We need to teach them Hebrew and values that will help them integrate into the movement's kibbutzim. I believe that if the children immigrate, their parents will join them. I'm now working on a plan for this coming year. We completed an initial survey these last few days of the three large nests: Lodz, Krakow and Statin, which is the biggest of them all. There are a few smaller nests, like in Lublin and Silesia. Altogether, there are five hundred and fifty members. We must double that number very shortly, complete training courses for counselors and turn the involvement in the nests into something attractive. We have to develop winter camps and summer camps. I know this is a fight for the souls of the youngsters since Yevsektsiya is doing everything in its power, even within the schools, to stop us. I need your help."

"How can I help?" Merie said.

"I'm practically working all alone. Most of the movement's leadership and members have already made *aliyah* to Israel. I can't run the program this way. I would like to enlist you as a consultant to the movement's top leadership. You have lots of experience and knowledge that none of those who are still here have. In order to consult with you I don't have to bring the entire leadership, it'll be enough if I come here. Also, two months ago, the Israeli embassy to Poland was opened headed by Yulik, Yisrael Barzelai, I'd like you to meet him."

"I know Yulik, I met him at the celebrations of the embassy's opening," Merie said. "How would you like the set-up to function?"

"I want to rent an apartment that will be a branch of the leadership in Warsaw, and here is where you come in. We need counselors, the best of the lot, in order to develop the movement in Poland. Some passports and visas and they want to make *aliyah* as quickly as possible and are about to join other movements that can immediately do that for them. It's a paradox. We are training the counselors and movement members for *aliyah*, but if they do so, we'll are left without counselors. That's the problem I'd like your help with."

"That's a unique *Shomer* trap, meaning that if you let them immigrate, you won't have anyone to train the others, and if you don't let them go, they will leave the movement anyway and there will be no counselors left and the movement will come to an end. Do you really think I'm the right person for solving such a problem?"

"Absolutely. Maybe you're the only one. I'll explain why. Anyone who wishes to immigrate to Israel has to get a passport and go through the Israeli embassy for a visa, which means coming to Warsaw. I will get Yulik on board so that without your signature and approval, he can't issue visas to our counselors. We will stipulate that any counselor, who submits a request to make *aliyah*, has to first meet with you in the leadership's apartment in Warsaw. To me, it's important that these meetings be held away from the nest's location. Your job will be to talk with them and to filter out those who must stay in Poland to keep the nest going. It is extremely important to have those counselors agree to stay, as they will have to continue their job highly motivated. I cannot have a staff of disappointed people. I believe you have the skills of being both empathic and assertive to convince the counselors that they cannot make *aliyah*, which is for the good of the movement as well as for their own. Yes, though it's a challenge, I am sure you can do it."

Merie remained silent, sensing the two men's intense look. "You know," she whispered, "that Rafal is about to be appointed director of the Polish Archives, directly under Prime Minister Cyrankiewicz. It is a unique position of trust. If, alongside his appointment, his wife becomes actively involved in the leadership of a movement, which today is legitimate but tomorrow might not be so and might even be hounded by the government, it could have serious repercussions on his life, on mine and the life of our children."

Merie paused, then added, "If I agree, Califf, it will be with two conditions: First, my name and role in the movement will remain secret, it will not be discussed in the leadership HQ, or mentioned in Poland or abroad."

"How can we present it to the counselors?" Califf asked.

"Tell them that before any decision is taken, they're being sent for a talk with an experienced member," Merie said.

"I accept your first condition," Califf said, "what is the second?"

"The second condition is that you guarantee to take me and my sons out of Poland immediately, legally or illegally, if and when I feel the time has come."

Alexander smiled and said, "I give my word that when we feel or you feel that it's the right time, we'll see to it that you and your family are taken out of Poland without delay, and every effort will be made that your husband won't learn of your activities with us, unless you yourself tell him."

Califf nodded. "Your contact will be with me alone. We will create a feasible cover for your visits to the movement's apartment and to your meetings with the counselors."

"Next week I'm going back to Israel," Alexander said. "I will be meeting with Shaul Avi Gur, who heads the illegal immigration alliance, and I will add your name to the highly exclusive list of *aliyah* activists. That way, you will be protected by the alliance when the time comes. We're also aware of your contribution to the organization in the messages passed to Berman."

"Okay," Merie said, "now if you can, I'll be grateful to hear from you what's happening in Israel, in the Jordan Valley, and in Shaar HaGolan."

"Because of the situation in Israel, my coming to Poland was postponed by a year," Califf said. "We too in kibbutz Aylon went through hard times. The war isn't over, but the second cease-fire since June 10 enabled tens of thousands of young people coming from Cyprus and the camps in Germany, to join the army, as for the massive flow of arms from Czechoslovakia. This set up many new army units that have changed the balance of power on the battlefield. The main thrust is to tackle the Egyptian army in the south and ensure an open route to Jerusalem. I believe that by next January, the war will end in our full victory and we will have far more territory than was designated to us by the UN General Assembly less than a year ago. We are not the ones who started the war, and the great number of our dead and wounded, is awful. But the outcome will allow us to open our gates to massive *aliyah* and create a real home for the Jewish people. As to Kibbutz Shaar HaGolan, I know that its members are still working hard at rebuilding it."

"Thank you, my friends, that's good news. I'm glad to meet you, Califf, and Alexander, I wish you a safe trip back home."

The two men left and Mary remained seated, thinking over the job she had just agreed to take upon herself.

Chapter Twelve:
The Children's Kibbutz Makes Aliyah To Israel

One week later, Merie came to the kibbutz to open the infirmary. "Good morning," Karieaski greeted her. "Could you please come to my room?"

"Did something happen?" Merie asked. It was not like Karieaski to invite her to his office.

"We're shutting down the kibbutz three days from now," he said taking their seat at his old desk.

"Three days? Why? What happened?" she asked, shocked.

"The Israeli embassy, the Youth Aliyah, the Jewish Agency and the movement came to an agreement with the Polish authorities, allowing all the children to leave for Israel immediately, closing the children's kibbutz. Two counselors from Israel have arrived and our staff and counselors are invited to join this coming Saturday and board the train that will take us to the Italian shoreline, from which we will sail to Israel."

"And what about me?" She asked. She always knew the day would come when the kibbutz would dismantle, yet now she felt a sudden sharp pain.

"You? You have a husband and two children, I assumed you'd make aliyah with them."

"I was joking," Merie said and stood up. "We'll go when the time is right for us. Now I have to be at the movement's apartment. I'll be back in two hours." She quickly left the room not looking at him as her eyes filled with tears.

Merie rushed to the movement's apartment where two pairs of counselors were waiting for her. A girl and a boy, both eighteen years old from Krakow and two boys from the Szczecin nest. In her preliminary discussion with the nest leader in Krakow, she understood that he didn't object to their leaving so she authorized their aliyah and stamped their request for a visa from the Israeli embassy. After they left, Yuzik and Noah entered. Merie listened to them and immediately understood she wouldn't be able to let them go. She was familiar with the terrible state the Szczecin nest was in.

"Why did you let the other two go and you're not letting us?" Yuzik asked angrily.

"I'm not preventing you from making aliyah, I'm simply asking you to wait a while longer so that the Szczecin nest doesn't fall apart. There's also the summer camp that's going to open on the Baltic shore in which the Szczecin nest will be involved in running it. The success of the camp is vital to the continued existence of our movement in Poland," she said. "We see this as an opportunity to expand our members vis a vis the summer camps sponsored by the Jewish committees linked to the Polish scout movement. Your cooperation is vital to the camp's success. When the camp ends, I can promise you I will authorize your aliyah to Israel, whether for one of you or both."

The two young men looked at one another and stood up. They shook hands with Merie and as they left, Califf walked in.

"I heard the last part of your talk with those two. You pulled it off beautifully. You refused them, yet they left content. I knew you'd do the job."

"Interesting that you should say that. I actually prefer to work with people but not manipulate them," Merie answered. "Now I have to get back to the children's kibbutz. I don't have much time left with them."

"In that case, I'll join you," Califf said.

They got on the tram to the children's kibbutz. Merie thought about the children. She knew that Boiruch had family in Israel, that Shloimele was an orphan and Dovid had an aunt in Tel Aviv. What about Rebecca? What will become of the girl who so completely won her heart?

Merie walked into the infirmary, the one place in which she felt most comfortable, whole with who she was. A nurse. She stared into space. She knew she couldn't put off her talk with Rafal much longer. He was so devoted to his new position in restoring the archives, that he would certainly refuse to leave Poland, but she and her sons could not stay here any longer.

"Merie, did you look for me?" Rebecca asked, walking in with a bright smile.

Merie spread out her arms and Rebecca ran into her embrace. They remained hugging one another when both Merie and Rebecca burst into tears. Merie wiped hers and Rebecca's faces. "No more crying, there's no reason to cry," Merie said.

"So why are you crying?" Rebecca asked.

"I'm sure you know that all of you are making aliyah to Israel this weekend."

Rebecca nodded. "And you're not?"

"You know I have a family here, a home, a husband and children."

"So we have to say goodbye?" Rebecca burst into tears again. "It's only because of you that I'm making aliyah."

"It's just for a short while, just a short while..." Merie hushed her. "We'd never leave you... Now go back to class. I'll see you again before you leave."

Karieaski knocked on the infirmary door and asked Merie to join him and Califf in the main lobby. All the children, thirty-four, were lined up in two rows and spotting Merie, they burst into loud applause and began singing a beloved Hebrew song in her honor. Her eyes welled up and when the singing ended, she went and hugged each child, stroking one's cheek, kissing another 6on his forehead, ruffling the hair of yet another. She then stood facing them. The room became silent and waiting for her to speak. Her emotional turmoil made her short of breath. Finally, she said, "Just this morning I was told that you are making aliyah to Israel. This is a great and happy day for you and for me. I will come to say goodbye on Saturday."

Chapter Thirteen:
The Meeting

"I have to prepare medical reports and medical files for each child," Merie said as she walked with Karieaski towards the infirmary. "There are children who are on medication. I suggest you appoint Anna and Zoshia to take charge of the medical treatment. I will instruct them how to take care of the children."

"Whatever you have to do in the infirmary, leave it for tomorrow," Karieaski said. "Meanwhile, as we're short of time, I would like you to accompany me to a meeting to discuss the movement's relationship with the *Hashomer Hatzair* political party, the Jewish committees and Poland's ruling party. I asked Califf for you to join our meeting with him and Barzelai and Meir Ye'ari. He's on his way to Paris and stopped here for a few days. I find us far too involved in the internal struggles between the movement, the party and the Jewish committees. I think listening to a non-political opinion is important."

"And am I supposed to support you and your views?"

"You're supposed to just listen to the different opinions and then express your own."

"Why wasn't I told about shutting down the kibbutz? I've been working with them for two years and they are very dear to me. I've treated every single child."

"The final decision was only taken yesterday. Since then, the matter of obtaining exit visas has been transferred from the Polish Foreign Office to the Interior Office, new exit visas are hardly approved these days. That's why, the moment the children's immigration was authorized, much to our surprise, we had to act quickly."

"Still, you could have let me know."

"You're right. That was a mistake. I'm sorry, I sincerely apologize."

"I'll join your meeting."

Califf hailed down a cab and gave him the address of the Israeli embassy.

Merie got into the cab and said, "If there are no exit visas, then why are we bothering to meet with the counselors who in any case can't leave Poland?"

"Their meetings with you instill some peace and quiet among the counselors, and quiet is what we need right now."

The embassy secretary led them to the boardroom, where Yisrael (Yulik) Barzelai and Meir Ye'ari were already waiting. They both stood up and shook hands.

"This is Merie Gerber," Califf said. "She is a member of our leadership as a consulter, and her connections with the movement as with the heads of the Jewish Committee and the Party, are worth hearing her input."

"Okay, then, let's start," Yisrael said.

"We've called this meeting to discuss the relationship between the educational movement, the Jewish committees and the *Hashomer Hatzair* political party," Califf began, shooting a defiant look at Barzelai and Ye'ari. 'He's certainly very sure of himself,' Merie thought.

"*Hashomer Hatzair* movement is fighting for its life here in Poland," he continued. "I believe that the most important, most ethical and most significant task facing the movement at this time, is to promote aliyah to Israel. The Polish government's objective is to restrict our educational activity in Poland, but we must fight that and refuse to accept it. The Jewish committees linked to the Communist Party are doing all they can to push us out of the schools, these are Jews that wish to integrate back into the Polish society. In the last committees convention we discovered that even the *Hashomer Hatzair* political party stands with them."

No one spoke.

"Califf," Barzelai said, "I am speaking now as a member of *Mapam*, the Socialist right wing of the United Workers Party, as a former *Hashomer Hatzair* member and as a member of Kibbutz Negba, but mainly as the Israeli ambassador and formal representative of our country in Poland. Things aren't that clear-cut. There is a Jewish community whose institutions are well organized that work hand in hand with the ruling party in Poland, to promote Jewish life in Poland. We cannot make light of the value of our connections with them and with the local government. We won't gain a thing by taking a combative stand. We must do everything we can to continue to nurture the Zionist idea and not lose the support of the remnant of the Jewish people in Poland. Let us not forget, in Poland there were three and a half million Jews, and today only seventy thousand remain. Can we truly look away? I don't believe we can do any such thing!"

"My friends," Ye'ari said, "there is another important aspect of the movement in Israel that is no less important. We in *Mapam* hold that it is of utmost importance to maintain contact with Soviet Russia and with the eastern European countries, especially Poland. During the War of Independence we fully understood the significance of this relationship." Ye'ari took a sip of his coffee, and then continued. "We are a Zionist and Socialist movement that waves two banners: Fulfillment of our pioneer spirit and aliyah to Israel, and fostering a progressive and

Socialist worldview. I expect to see an end to the power struggles and ideological battles with the Jewish committees and the Communist Party's Yevsektsiya."

Barzelai and Califf remained silent.

"In my opinion, any discussion on this matter will become irrelevant in a few months' time, because of processes that are now unfolding that are beyond our or your control," Merie said.

"What processes?" Ye'ari asked.

"I spent eight years in the Soviet Union," Merie said. "Their interest lies in spreading their hegemony on the eastern European countries, particularly Poland and Czechoslovakia, that seemingly still maintain some semblance of a pluralistic democracy. I believe the Zionist youth movements, and the Jewish parties as well, will be eradicated within a few months' time, regardless of whether you're nice to them or not." Merie took a deep breath, and then continued. "I'm sure you know that my husband was one of the founders of the Union of Polish Patriots in Russia. This union was the Communist reaction to the right-wing Polish government-in-exile based in London, and founded the pro-Soviet rule in Poland. I recall that as early as 1943, they were holding discussions on post-war Poland. The Union of Patriots sought a nation state and not a multinational one that existed before the war. And lo and behold, after the war ended and the new borders were set, they transferred more than four million Germans to Germany and a quarter of a million Ukrainians to the Ukraine. They did the same with the people of Belarus. Most of the Jews who returned from Russia to Poland through the repatriation agreements, joined the escape movement to Israel passing through the misplaced persons camps in Germany. All this was done to preserve an absolute majority of Poles, and preserve one Polish language and culture. These processes are nearing the end. If anyone thinks they will allow the continued existence of pioneer Hebrew-speaking youth movements or active Zionist Jewish political parties, then he's sorely mistaken."

"What do you suggest then?" Barzelai asked.

"To encourage anyone who can leave to make aliyah, once the gates are opened, and especially," she looked at Ye'ari, "to be prepared for their absorption in Israel, so that this wave of aliyah won't flood the American shores."

"And what about you, Merie?" Califf asked.

"I will help you as best I can, and when the gates open, my sons and I will pass through them."

"What about your husband?" Barzelai asked.

"When the time comes, he will have to make a choice."

"I suggest that we put a stop to the internal and external wars and see in which direction the wind is blowing," Barzelai summed up the meeting and Merie and Califf left.

"We'll take a cab to your house and we can talk on the way," Califf said.

"I hope I didn't ruin things for you," Merie said. "You told me I could express my opinion and that's what I did."

"This was an important meeting and what you brought up was some perspective and common sense. What are the politicians from the Zionist parties fighting about? The seating arrangements on stage when the unity ceremony is held? If everything is about to disappear, what's the point of all this fighting?"

Merie nodded. "So now, with the children leaving, what next?"

"We have the summer camp ahead of us. You can help with the planning and organization of the scouts unit and the graduates' unit. It will be held on the Baltic seashore and you can bring your boys with you." Merie smiled as she stepped out of the cab, noticing Rafal who had just arrived home.

"Rafal," she called out, "I want you and Califf to meet. He heads the leadership of *Hashomer Hatzair* in Poland. We met at the children's kibbutz as he told us that the children and their staff are making aliyah this coming Saturday." Rafal didn't respond. When... when will she tell him that the time has come?

Chapter Fourteen:
Summer Camp

At exactly twelve noon on Saturday, the children waved goodbye from the train. Merie remained standing on the platform, feeling sad. With the closing of the kibbutz, she plunged into organizing the summer camp for the older movement's members on the Baltic seashore.

All the while, she continued her meetings with counselors who wanted to expedite their aliyah to Israel.

After ending a meeting with two girl counselors from the Szczecin nest, held at the Movement's apartment, Califf walked in. "Hi Merie," he said. "How are things going with the preparations for the summer camp?"

"They're going well. As you know, the director, Yosef Mann's attempts to lease the guesthouse north of Szczecin on the Baltic shore fell through. Instead, a farm was leased in Karwia, a seaside town. It has a large guest house near the beach and two villas that used to serve as summer homes for German military and political VIPs." This brought a smile to Califf's face. "I'll help Yosef in running the camp and will be responsible for the health issues," Merie continued. "Plans are that the first week will be devoted to fun and relaxation, with lots of activities on the beach. In the afternoons, after lunch and a rest, we'll hold *Hashomer* activities, and in evenings parties and folk dancing. Misha and his accordion have been recruited for that. During the second week, more time will be devoted to educational activities, lectures and group discussions, but we'll still spend time on the beach. The third week will be taken up mostly with a scouting game, which will be held in the nearby forest, and we will sum up with activities and discussions on aliyah to Israel and individual fulfillment. We will hold a special farewell ceremony with the closing of the summer camp. My sons, Alec and Edjic, are so excited."

"I'm glad to hear how the plans are taking shape," Califf said. "Among the movement's summer projects, the summer camp is clearly the pivot in the viability and growth of the movement next year. The youth movement of the Jewish Committee is also running summer camps, so we must rise to the challenge and be better than them."

That evening, at the dinner table, Merie said, not looking at her husband: "I was invited to join the staff of *Hashomer Hatzair*'s summer camp in Karwia, north of Gdansk."

"And you accepted?" Rafal asked, raising his eyebrows.

"I did," Merie said looking directly at him. "It's a three-week summer vacation for me and the boys at the seashore. What's wrong with that?"

"Don't you think you should have discussed this with me first?" Rafal asked.

"Perhaps, but you've been so busy with your new job."

Alec and Edjic raised their hands with cries of joy. "We're going to the beach! We're going to the beach!"

"What would you prefer?" Merie asked, smiling. "That I leave the boys with you for the summer?"

Rafal chuckled. "You've pulled one over me, haven't you, Merie Gerber?" he said. "Okay, let it be, but next time, I'm sure you will be able to find the right time to share information regarding my children with me."

The train headed for the seashore town of Gdansk was packed with seventy-two boys and girls from *Hashomer Hatzair* who came together from all parts of Poland. Their loud, cheerful voices expressed their excitement at going to summer camp. Alec and Edjic were sitting in the conductor's room, telling him all about the summer camp they were going to.

When the train reached Gdansk, the campers and the staff left for the camp in five trucks with one loaded with equipment and food supplies that had been purchased in Gdansk. Merie and Edjic sat near the driver, while Alec sat with the campers in the back.

The farm consisted of a central building that served as the camp's administration offices and the administration staff's quarters. The children were lodged in the barns, rather than in the villas where the heads of the Nazi party stayed.

The Baltic Sea spread out along the wide, golden beach, inviting the young campers to take a dip. The moist, salty air made many of them giggly and over-energetic as they helped unload the food and equipment from the truck.

Merie checked out the large, inviting rooms of the main building. "You couldn't have found a better place than this for the summer camp," she said to Yosef.

"Wait. You still haven't seen the amazing seashore, and the forest that is so perfectly suited to our third week's activities. It's as if this place has been set up especially for us. The cursed Germans, damn them, knew how to build an exquisite farm."

"I was anxious about bringing my little boy with me, but now I see him running around with the older children, so happy even with sixteen-year-olds," she giggled. "I hope we get the older adolescent level to run the camp. Remember, we agreed to interfere only when needed."

"In that case, all that's left for us to do is to enjoy ourselves," Yosef said.

The warm weather and the carefree atmosphere lifted the spirits of them all. Most of the time, the campers walked around in shorts and sleeveless tops, which was a new experience for them.

On the second day, funny boxing matches were held on the beach. The highlight was a boxing match between Edjic and Yosef, the camp director. All the campers stood around them in a circle, watching closely. At the end of the first round, the match ended with Yosef on the ground and to the loud cheers of the campers, Edjic was declared camp champion.

For most of the campers, this was their first time at the beach. On the fourth day, Shimel, a young camper went into the water, not knowing how to swim. He started swallowing water and began to drown. Alec, who noticed that rushed into the water, swam to him, and pulled him out. Yosef and Merie were on the beach, they lay him on his side, pressed his belly, until he spewed out the water he had swallowed, and Merie had him taken to the camp infirmary.

"You did something very important, Alechico," Merie said. "Weren't you afraid you too would be caught in the tide? After all, Shimel is bigger and heavier than you."

"No, I wasn't afraid. I saw he needed help so I immediately jumped in."

"Next time, just call for help," Merie said and hugged him. She felt her heart bursting with pride in her son's courage and daring.

After the drowning incident with Shimel, the campers' entry into the sea was limited. While on campgrounds, the counselors concentrated on leading educational activities, and delegates from Israel arrived to tell them about the War of Independence and how the movement's kibbutzim protected the new homeland. Califf also came to visit, and all the campers gathered in the central building to listen to him.

"*Shomrim*, strength!" Califf began.

"Strength and courage!" They called back with the movement's cry.

"Friends," Califf began, "We are a movement whose values are socialistic, a movement that believes in world brotherhood. But just as important, we are part of the Jewish people. We believe that the Jewish people can fulfill its destiny only in its own land, in *Eretz Yisrael*. Kibbutzim exist only in Israel, not in North America, not in Australia, not in Europe, not in Poland. Four years and three months have passed since the Second World War ended. A war in which six million Jews were murdered. In Israel's War of Independence, which ended only a few months ago, six thousand soldiers found died. What did they die for? For us – Never again! Never again will Jews march to the gas chambers. This is the time to make aliyah to Israel." Califf's eyes swept over each camper. "Are my words understood?"

"Understood, Comrade Califf!"

"In the past few months, the Polish authorities stopped issuing exit visas and right now there are discussions initiated by Israel's embassy to open the gates. A decision will be made in a few days. If the gates are opened to leave Poland, we will have to get organized for a quick exit. I wish to add that the absorption process in Israel is not easy. We lack many resources. However, the Israelis' arms are wide open to receive you. Next week we will initiate a game that will summarize your three-week stay in this camp. I will come for the closing ceremony and hope that by then we will be better informed. Till then, *shomrim*, strength!"

"Strength and courage!" Everyone called.

Califf left the building, pulling out a handkerchief from his pocket and wiping his brow. Merie and Yosef saw him to

Yosef's office, where they waited for his cab to arrive and take him back to Gdansk.

"Was that an 'end of the world' speech?" Merie joked.

"Not far from it. I don't really know if I'll be seeing this great group of kids again. I'm afraid I'm no longer in the know as to what's happening behind the scenes. That's why I felt it was so important to introduce into their young hearts and minds that there is no other alternative but to make aliyah to Israel."

"Well, you succeeded," Yosef said. "I hope you can make it to our closing ceremony and speak to them again."

"I'll try," Califf answered as he headed for the cab. "And what about you? If the gates open, will you be coming?" He asked Merie.

"I believe nothing will stop me from making aliyah to Israel this time," she replied. "Poland is not my home. I don't want my children to grow up here. Still, I don't know if Rafal will agree to join us. And if he does, will he be able to do so? Will the Poles let him go?"

"I understand," Califf said. "Whatever decision you make, it will involve some sacrifice." He hugged her as he got into the cab.

On Saturday evening, all the campers and staff gathered in the central hall. "We have come to the third and last week of camp," Yosef said, looking at the sun-tanned children. "This week will sum up everything we have done so far and play the great scouting game. You will be divided into two camps, blue and red. The blue camp will be called the North Pioneers, or in short, 'the northerners.' And the red camp will be called the 'Southern Pathfinders,' or in short, 'the southerners.' Each group member will receive a colored ribbon that you will tie to your wrist or your forehead. Alec will give out the blue ribbons and Edjic will give out the red ones. It's important that each of you knows which group he or she belongs to. Six campers will be the referees. They will wear yellow ribbons. Three referees will join each team. The red and blue areas will be separated by a forest path. The blue group includes members or graduates from the nests in Lodz, Krakow and Chentakhova, and the red group members and graduates from the nests in Szczecin, Ludwikow and the young adults' kibbutz. After receiving your ribbons, each group will sit separately and the referees with the yellow ribbons will join you."

Everyone started talking at once, but Yosef raised his hand and said, "Quiet! I will now explain the rules of the game. The blue group will build a 'Tower and Stockade' settlement – Hanita, in the blue area in the forest. The red group will build a 'Tower and Stockade' settlement – Negba, in the red area in the forest. Both settlements will be built in one day. Failing to do so, they will be destroyed by the 'yellows', the British referees." Yosef smiled.

"The game will start on Tuesday evening, then each group will go to its area and build the settlement. Each group will build a ten-foot tower from wooden beams tied together with ropes. Two tents will also be constructed on either side of the tower, and a rope running along each area, three feet above ground, with small flags attached to it will mark each area's borders and will symbolize the wall. In order to reach the site and build the settlement, the pioneers must evade the 'yellows.' Once the settlement's constructions are approved, a blue flag will be flown from the tower in Hanita and a red flag from the Negba tower.

At night, the second stage will begin. Each group will be subdivided into protectors and raiders. The protectors will protect the kibbutz settlement, while the raiders, called 'Palmachniks' in the blue group and 'Samson's foxes' in the red group, will have to steal the flag from the other group and bring it to their camp. The first group to steal the flag from the other one will be the winner. You're familiar with all the other rules from our movement's game, Our Flag. If a protector touches a raider, this means he's caught. If there are some details you're not clear about or you have questions, ask the referees, they will make the final decision. Good luck to both groups."

Preparations for the game and for the fire marks for the closing ceremony took two days, and on Tuesday afternoon, the two groups left for their mission – building a settlement. By evening both groups had built 'tower and stockade' kibbutzim. The red and blue flags were raised and a timeout was called.

As night fell, the campers took their places along the path that divided the two groups, ready to raid the other group and steal its flag. At one a.m., the blue raiders from the north entered the southerners' Negba settlement, but were spotted and had to get back to their camp. An hour later, the red raiders from Negba invaded the northern Hanita camp, and all its members gathered in the center of the red settlement and started to shout "Out! Out!" chasing the invaders out. The fast runners headed for the border but were caught by the better 'red' defenders. Only Shmil walked slowly. No one believed that the red flag was hidden in his pants. When he crossed the border between the two camps, he started sprinting waving the flag. Everyone from the 'blue' group cheered and yelled, 'We won! We won!"

The following evening, the closing ceremony was held. Califf arrived a few moments earlier while the campers, counselors and staff were already standing in line, facing the fire sign, 'Fear not! Be strong!'

The excitement was tangible. "The summer camp was a great success," Yosef began. He congratulated the 'blue' group on its victory and complimented the 'red' group for its efforts. "I would like to thank all those who invested and contributed to the success of this camp. The movement is expecting to see you leading next year. We hope to double and even triple the number of members and make *Hashomer Hatzair* a leading Jewish youth movement in Poland. Now, I'd like to call upon Califf, head of the movement's leadership, to say a few words."

Califf stood facing the straight lines of campers and called out in a loud voice, "*Shomrim*, strength!"

"Strength and courage!" The campers responded.

Califf paused for a long moment, then said, "I'm sorry, but all that won't happen," and turned to look at Yosef. There was absolute silence, and the campers looked at one another, puzzled. This wasn't the Califf they knew.

"This morning, there was an announcement in an official Warsaw newspaper that all the Jews in Poland are free to submit a request for an exit visa to Israel," he said. "The authorization is valid till August of next year. After that, no requests for exit visas from Poland will be authorized. This means that the hold put on leaving Poland has now been lifted." A buzz of excitement spread through the crowd. "But that isn't all that I want to share with you," Califf continued. "An unequivocal message was sent to Israel's ambassador and to all the Zionist and non-Zionist movements and parties asking them to fully dismantle, they will be closed. By the end of this year, 1949, no *Hashomer Hatzair* or any other Jewish youth movement will exist in Poland." Califf looked at Yosef, who was in shock, and said in a quiet voice, "I'm so sorry, but they won't be counselors in *Hashomer Hatzair* in Poland. They will make aliyah to Israel." He looked at the campers once again. "Return to your homes," he said. "Talk with your parents, and with your relatives. We will do everything we can to help in your moving to Israel. Those whose families wish to stay in Poland, we will help make aliyah through the youth groups in the Movement's kibbutzim. We will meet again on December 31, with all those who will stay in Poland. We will march through the ruins of the Warsaw ghetto to No. 18 Mila Street, just as we marched this year to the memorial statue of the ghetto uprising. We will then announce the end of the Movement's activities." In a quiet voice, Califf added, "*Shomrim*, strength!"

The campers responded weakly, "Strength and courage!"

Chapter Fifteen:
Decisions

On the train ride back to Warsaw, Merie was deep in thought. The children kept their distance, they sensed that she needed her space and quiet. Making aliyah to Israel meant breaking up the family, she knew that. But should she relinquish her dream that was always part of her life, ever since her high school days at *Tarbut* Gymnasia?

When the train pulled into Warsaw station, the children ran to Rafal who was waiting for them on the platform, climbing all over him. They all spoke together, rushing to share with him their experiences from the summer camp. Merie stood aside, waiting for their joy and excitement to subside, then offered her cheek to Rafal. He immediately sensed her anger. "What happened?" He asked.

"We'll talk at home," she replied heading to the exit. A porter carried their suitcases and Rafal followed her to the cab that was waiting outside. They rode in silence the entire way home to 16 Konopazka Street. When they entered the apartment, Alec and Edjic wasted no time rushing outside to play with their friends.

"Why didn't you tell me what your Yevsektsiya is up to?" She was furious. "The papers published the news that now all the Jews can apply for exit visas to Israel, that this arrangement will last only till next August and next year no Jewish youth movements or political parties will be allowed."

"As far as I know, the heads of the Yevsektsiya asked for approval to exit Poland only for the Zionist leadership, the anti-government intellectuals and the religious Jews. No one expected to see such sweeping permission to leave Poland. The announcement in the papers came as a complete surprise."

"I see," Merie said. "Till the end of this year the boys and I are making aliyah to Israel. That's my final decision. You can join us or not, as you wish."

"What's the rush? We have an entire year to decide. There's no need to hurry."

"What you told me just reinforced my feelings that I can't trust your party. Whoever surprised you once can surprise you and me again with a counter-decision. I want you to come with us to Israel, and if you can't and aren't interested in joining us, then at least contact all your connections so that we can leave as soon as possible."

"I will not give up the children and you know very well that I can't leave my present position."

"You promised you wouldn't stand in my way when I decide to make aliyah."

"And how will you live? How will you support our children? Hundreds of thousands of immigrants are swarming into Israel from the camps. Everyone has to be fed... you will starve... wasn't Tashkent enough for you? You were so thin, I was afraid you would die."

"I won't be lacking for food."

"What makes you so sure of that?"

"I'm a nurse. I can always find work and support our children, anywhere."

"Yes, but if you work, who will look after them?"

"I'm planning to join Kibbutz Shaar HaGolan in the Jordan Valley. There, children are under the care of *metaplot*, caregivers, while the parents can work, and in the afternoons, the children are with the parents. Nahum Boneh, Pola and my friends from Pinsk live there. They'll be glad to accept me and the boys."

"Shaar HaGolan? The kibbutz that the Syrians torched a year ago? Do you hear what you're saying? In Tashkent you were so critical of the Communist inefficiency, in Moscow you criticized the Communist government, you're not ready to have your children grow up in Warsaw, and in Israel you'll live on a kibbutz? I heard that you went behind my back and worked with the Aliyah organization."

Merie remained silent. "I was always a few steps ahead of you. Just like when we escaped from the German army in '41. If it were up to you, we would have stayed in Kiev and killed in Babi Yar. The same thing in Kharkov and Stalingrad on our way to Tashkent."

Rafal dropped down on the couch, holding his head between his hands. In all their confrontations, she always had the upper hand, but somehow things later followed his wishes. This time he knew he had been defeated. "If you have already checked and decided, then what do you want?"

Merie sat down next to him. "I love you," she said. "You're my husband and the father of my children and I don't want to divorce you. I just want to leave Poland. When you will be able to leave, I will welcome you with open arms. Meanwhile, I'm asking for your help to get our exit visas. Rafal, I know, and you know too, that if you want to come with us, you can."

Rafal began pacing the room. Merie looked at him anxiously. "This is so hard," he said. "The attitude of the Polish leadership to Israel and the Zionist movements is changing and I agree that perhaps in the near future, the movements will face greater difficulties. I think that it's for your good and the good of the children that..." He paused, and then continued. "I will ask for you to be granted a visa to visit relatives in Israel, good for one year. At the end of that time, you don't have to return to Poland. In the meantime, I'll be able to ask for a travel visa to visit you there, because formally you will still be considered Polish citizens."

Merie was happy yet sad. What she had always wanted was now happening, but the price she and her sons have to pay is very high. Yet not as high as living in a country that is not your home, she told herself decisively.

5.

ISRAEL

Chapter One: Aliyah: Immigrating To Israel

U p to the end of November 1949, thirty thousand requests were submitted from Polish Jews for exit visas to Israel, and as November came to a close, the exit visas for Merie and her two sons arrived. Through the communication network of the aliyah organization, Merie informed Nahum Boneh that she was leaving Poland in early December. Nahum confirmed her joining the kibbutz.

As the time came closer, Merie placed a large wooden chest on their balcony and she, along with Rafal and the boys, packed all their clothing, linens and house utensils they would need during their first few years in the new land. In a suitcase and a bag, she packed all they would need on their two-week voyage to Israel on board a ship. Merie recalled her long journeys on the trains in Russia running away from the Germans, with Alec in her arms. Now she isn't running, she told herself. There are people waiting for her there in Israel.

The wooden chest was sealed and shipped to Kibbutz Shaar HaGolan. The aliyah organization informed them that they must reach Bari in southern Italy, where a transit camp was set up for immigrants from Europe who would then leave on immigration ships to Israel. The ship *Kedma* was scheduled to sail out of Bari on December 14, and another ship, *Galila*, was sailing out on December 21st. Merie decided she would leave Poland on December 13.

Rafal, his beloved sister Toshya, her husband Felik and friends from the Jewish Committee and *Hashomer Hatzair* came to the train station to say goodbye to Merie and the children. Merie and Rafal stood aside in a quiet corner. "Come...I'll be waiting for you," she whispered. Rafal held her close choked.

The last whistle was heard. Merie and the two boys boarded the train. "My darlings," Merie said to her sons who were still over-excited from the leave-taking. "We are on our way to Israel, and it's a very long journey, so please try to be good." They nodded enthusiastically and Merie hugged them both, nestling her head between them. She had escaped from Warsaw and now she was leaving it behind.

That evening, the train pulled into Katowice where they changed trains, taking a midnight train to Bratislava in Czechoslovakia. For the train to climb the steep Tatra Mountains, it needed two locomotives, one in the front, pulling, and one in the back, pushing. As soon as the train pulled out, snow began to fall, and the further south they traveled, the heavier the snow became. The front locomotive snowplowed the snow so the train advanced slowly. After a short but rough struggle between the brothers, Alec climbed up to the top bunk and Edjic remained on the bottom and they quickly dropped off.

Merie sat on her bed, awash with adrenalin. Here she is, on her way to her homeland with her children, she is living her dream as it is turning into reality. Did she do the right thing? Will her children be able to integrate into kibbutz life? Will they learn Hebrew quickly? Will she find her place?

The train chugged up the mountains and at noon it reached the Barno station, the back locomotive was removed. Towards evening, they reached Bratislava and once again had to change trains. Czech border patrol police together with secret service men in civilian clothes, passed from one passenger to the next, checking their suitcases, asking the purpose of their travel. Few passengers were taken off the train and driven to the secret service offices for further questioning.

In the evening, the train was cleared to cross the border but then the Austrian border police walked in. "Welcome to Austria" they smiled at the passengers. In Vienna, once again Merie and the boys switched trains and boarded a train that headed for Graz and Klagenfurt. The higher the train climbed in the mountains, the stronger the snowstorm became. When they reached a mountain pass, the snow had blocked its entrance and they had to wait for a full day until it was cleared.

The following day the sun came out. Before them spread a vista of pure white slopes and granite cliffs of the Italian Dolomites. In the late hours of the night, the train pulled into Padova. That night Merie and the boys slept in a hotel close to the station, and the following morning she exchanged their tickets for first class. The train pulled out towards evening and they all boys fell asleep immediately, exhausted.

They woke up to the warm Italian sun. To their left the Adriatic Sea spread in all its glory and to their right, green fields extended out to the horizon. That evening they arrived in Bari. At the train station, representatives of the Jewish Agency who were excited to hear Merie speak fluent Hebrew, met them. "The *Kedma* sailed out two days ago," the agent told her. "And the *Galila* is due at the port in three days. You can go to the transit immigrant camp, or if you have the means, we can show you the Contini guest house, where you will get a room at a low rate with three meals a day." Merie chose the guesthouse, where she spent the last days before sailing. In her mind, she heard Gudel saying, "I told you, you can do it!" Before she fell asleep, her mother whispered in her ear, "You'll see, Merie, everything will work out fine."

The ship *Galila* pulled into port on the evening of December 20 and the following morning, Merie and the children rushed over to see it. Merie's disappointment was obvious. *Galila* looked more like a riverboat floating down the Vizsla. "How can hundreds of passengers sail in that?" She asked an Agency worker.

"It's a small boat, but it already did several rounds from Bari to Haifa and back," he said. Merie bit her lips. In the evening, she and the boys boarded. In the hull of the ship, metal poles were installed, throughout and between them three levels of tarpaulin sheets were stretched that served as bunks. Merie found two beds for her and Edjic on the bottom level and one for Alec on the higher one. Alec liked the challenge of climbing up there and Edjic envied him but forgot all about it when the ship met its first storm. Everyone was told to clear the deck and get down to the ship's belly, and the crew quickly tied down whatever cargo was left on deck. "This is a high-grade storm," they were told. "You're best off lying in bed so as not to fall and get hurt." Within minutes many passengers began throwing up. Merie felt nauseous but her bigger concern was for Edjic who couldn't stop vomiting. Alec, on the other hand, enjoyed the rocking of the boat and didn't seem to be affected by the storm.

The following morning the sun came out the sea turned blue and smooth. After the passengers went up to the deck, the crew came in with water pipes to clean the floors. On deck, two long lines formed for the toilets: the men's line and a much longer line of the women, where Merie stood. She recalled Rafal's words:

"Where are you rushing to with two small children? Wasn't the war enough for you, all the suffering and hunger and escaping..." If he could see her and his two sons now, he would say, "Well, is this what you wished for, for your sons?"

The lovely day that followed the storm quickly passed. As the ship approached Crete, it once again encountered a storm far stronger and longer than the previous one. Merie felt so sick, she was unable to bring Edjic to the upper deck to vomit and put Alec in charge of him. Alec dragged his brother up the steep steel steps to the deck and later washed his face.

On the morning of December 25, the *Galila* drew close to the breakwater of Haifa harbor. The passengers gathered on the deck, hoping to catch sight of the Carmel Mountain, but instead were greeted by torrential rain and low grey clouds.

"We've come to Israel," Merie exclaimed and hugged Alec and Edjic. A shiver ran down her spine.

Chapter Two:
The Gateway To Aliyah

Merie always dreamt of Israel and its blue skies and sunny days, but now, on her first day she was welcomed by a full-blown Israeli winter. A line of trucks covered with tarpaulin, waited on the harbor's platform to carry the ship's passengers to the *Shaar Haaliyah* absorption camp, which provided housing for immigrants during their first days in Israel. Merie and her sons were placed in a spacious military tent along with other families that had arrived on the boat with them. The rain didn't stop and the campgrounds turned into a huge muddy mush, with wooden walkways between the tents.

Towards evening, they got to a tent to meet with the Jewish Agency and the Absorption Service people. Two men sat behind a long table. "Welcome. I'm Yoel. Please, have a seat," said one of the men in Polish. "I'm a Jewish Agency representative and this is Moshe, representative of the Absorption Services."

"Shalom. My name is Merie Gerber and these are my sons, Alec and Edjic," Merie answered in Hebrew and giggled at the amazed expression on the men's faces. "I speak Hebrew," she smiled. "Could you please contact Kibbutz Shaar HaGolan and inform Nahum Boneh at the kibbutz that I've arrived?"

"We can do that," Yoel said.

"Thank you. Could you also please contact the office of the illegal immigration alliance and let them know I'm here in Israel?"

The two men exchanged looks. Moshe left the room and Yoel continued going over the documents Merie had brought with her from Poland. Nearly an hour later, Moshe returned. "Your requests have been granted," he said. "I informed the immigration office and they will send delegates tomorrow to meet with you. I also spoke with the secretary of Kibbutz Shaar HaGolan, and after the medical procedures are completed, they will come to take you to the kibbutz. We will do everything we can to speed up the process and have you leave the day after tomorrow. Welcome home, Mrs. Gerber."

At the break of dawn, the sun's first rays made their appearance and the skies were a clear blue. A volunteer named Shoshana entered the tent and said, "Good morning, I will be escorting you along the absorption chain. First, we will have breakfast in the dining room, then start the citizenship process and give you an identification card. After that, you will go through medical checkups and finally will get your membership number for the public health system."

Merie received a blue ID card and after a general checkup, blood tests and chest x-rays, everyone was asked to undress for a disinfection treatment with yellow DDT powder. "Don't feel bad," Merie said when she noticed the pity on Shoshana's face. "I was a nurse at an orphanage in Tashkent, where we also used these methods."

When the intake process ended, the family returned to the bustling tent. The children played outside with their new friends and Merie lay down on her bed. Shoshana came in. "Come," she said. "There's someone waiting for you."

"Alec, keep an eye on Edjic please, till I return," Merie said, and the two women walked towards the absorption cabins. Three men were sitting at the table: Moshe, Alexander and a third man. Merie was thrilled to finally see someone she knew and rushed to hug Alexander.

"Merie," Alexander said, "this is Shaul, he is one of the directors of the Mossad. The illegal immigration alliance doesn't exist anymore and now transporting immigrants to Israel has been handed over to the Shoham Company, a subsidiary of the Zim Company that operates the ships, including the *Galila*. From now on, we are known as the Mossad and we will be responsible, among others, to organize aliyah to Israel from the eastern European countries."

Shaul joined in: "We've initiated this meeting in order to tell you how appreciative we are of your activities in Warsaw for the past two years. I wish to tell you that the current government, the first government of the State of Israel, has decided to grant aliyah activists with special absorption conditions. The contribution made by you and many others to the escape, to rebuilding youth movements in the diaspora and encouraging aliyah to Israel, has been immense and you are a full partner in the establishment of the State of Israel."

Merie nodded her head slightly and said, "Thank you for your kind words."

"As a token of our appreciation," Shaul continued, "the government has decided to grant the aliyah activists with an apartment free of charge, and a work position wherever they choose to settle down. I am here to inform you that you have been designated as an aliyah activist and are entitled to these benefits following the government's decision."

Merie smiled. "I thank you so much," she said, "but I prefer to join my friends at Kibbutz Shaar HaGolan. Nahum Boneh will be coming tomorrow to take us to the kibbutz."

"We respect your decision," Shaul said and shook her hand.

"How did Rafal react to your making aliyah?" Alexander asked when they walked out of the cabin. "Is he planning to join you?"

"I don't know," Merie said. "The decision is up to him."

Alexander gazed at her. "You've made the right decision," he said.

"I think so too," Merie said. She then turned to Shaul. "Tell me, Shaul, how many of us have been designated aliyah activists in Poland?"

"A hundred and thirty-two," Shaul replied.

"And how many of them chose to live in a kibbutz?"

"Seven," he said with a smile. "And you're the eighth."

"Then apparently we're a rare species, aren't we?"

"It appears so," he said. "Good luck to you and your boys. If you change your mind, you know how to find us."

The following day the sun shone again, and in the early afternoon hours, a pickup truck from the kibbutz arrived. Nahum Boneh stepped out and welcomed Merie and her two boys. They got into the back of the pickup truck and sat on benches facing one another. The truck left the Shaar HaAliyah camp and headed towards Haifa, and from there to Kibbutz Shaar HaGolan.

On December 31, the last youth members of *Hashomer Hatzair* in Poland marched to No.18 Mila Street in Warsaw. At the foot of the mound of ruins of the building in which the last heroic battle took place by the Warsaw Ghetto fighters, Califf read aloud: "As of tomorrow, the *Hashomer Hatzair* movement in Poland will cease to exist. We shall meet in our homeland, Israel."

EPILOGUE

Merie worked as a nurse in Kibbutz Shaar HaGolan and in the Schweitzer Hospital in Tiberias and as a public health nurse until the late 1950s. In the summer of 1958, she traveled with her son Edjic, who had changed his name to Ehud, to Warsaw for a three-month visit to examine the future of her relationship with Rafal. They decided that he would stay in Israel for a year and try to get a professorship at the university. Merie left the kibbutz, rented an apartment in Tel Aviv and worked as a nurse in a public health clinic. In 1960, Rafal arrived in Israel, but could not find his place there. They divorced and he returned to Poland.

During her years as a nurse, Merie was sent by the Jewish Agency to the transit absorption camps in Europe. In the late 1960s, she helped in the absorption of new immigrants from Romania stationed in the transit camp in Naples. In the early 1970s, she took part in the absorption of new immigrants from Morocco in the transit camp in Marseilles, and in the mid-1970s she helped with the absorption of new immigrants from Russia, in the transit camp in Vienna.

Merie retired in the late 1970s but continued working as a nurse almost up to her last days. Alec specialized in urban transportation planning and for most of his life lived with his family in Har Adar, in the Judean Mountains, working in the Transportation Ministry. Edjic changed his first name to Ehud and his surname to Regev. He worked as an economic advisor and company manager and lives with his family in the community of Rishpon.

Merie died on December 17, 1986, in Ichilov Hospital in Tel Aviv. Today, on that same floor where Merie drew her last breath, is the spine surgery department, where her grandson, Dr. Gilad Regev, is a senior doctor, orthopedist and spine surgeon and a director of the Minimally Invasive Spine Surgery Service.

ACKNOWLEDGEMENTS

I wish to thank the many people who helped, supported and encouraged me in writing this book.

First, to **my wife Yehudit**, who was there for me from the very first day of writing. She read, corrected and expressed her opinion on every single chapter.

To **Rotem Biron**, who worked diligently on turning my manuscript into a readable and flowing book.

To **Professor Aviva Halamish**, who contributed her extensive knowledge of the historic period this book covers, and for her willingness to read and comment on the first draft.

To **Tzipi Yaakov**, my teacher in Creative Writing and Writing Life Stories at the Open University, who read, enlightened and commented even after the course ended.

To **Alon El-Gar** of blessed memory, **my brother Alec**, who strained his memory to recall and tell me about his life experiences in Tashkent, Moscow and Warsaw.

To **Dr. Gilad Regev**, orthopedic specialist and spine surgeon at Ichilov Hospital, for his help with the medical data.

To **Dr. Dalia Regev** for her help with the chemistry data.

To **my sons**, **Shay** and **Benny Regev**, who read the first draft and whose comments helped bring major topics into focus.

To **Dr. Ruth Broida**, of blessed memory, **Prof. Matityahu Mintz**, of blessed memory, and **Prof. Eli Tzur** for their rich and knowledgeable contribution to understanding the historic background of the book.

To **Prof. Shimon Rodnitzki**, at the History Department, Warsaw University, Poland.

To **Prof. Arieh and Chana Kroglenski** for their help for their contacts in Warsaw; to **Olga Koblatzok**, for her great help in organizing my visit to Warsaw and my work there; and to **Nili Amit** from the Jewish Museum in Warsaw who accompanied our visit there.

To everyone who encouraged, asked questions and waited with anticipation to see this book come to light.

And of course, to **my mother**, **Merie**, a true hero, whose personality and actions have been only partially described in this book. Were it not for her determination and strength, I would not be here to tell her story through this book.

GLOSSARY OF NAMES AND EVENTS

THE MOLOTOV-RIBBENTROP PACT – a non-aggression pact between Nazi Germany and Communist Russia (signed in Moscow on 23 August 1939) on the division of Poland close to the outbreak of World War II.

THE YALTA CONFERENCE – Held in February 1945 in Livadia Palace, in Yalta, Crimea, towards the end of World War II, with the participation of Stalin, Churchill and Roosevelt, in which spheres of influence in Europe were divided with the war's end between the Soviet Union and the West.

ARMIA KRAJOWA (AK) [Kariova] – Army of the People, the largest underground movement of the Polish resistance during World War II. After the war ended, the AK was dismantled and in its stead a secret movement began, called NIE, which is the first part of the Polish word for 'Independence.'

HASHOMER HATZAIR – The first secular Jewish, Zionist youth movement. Established in 1913 in southeast Poland. Within several years, it spread to hundreds of nests throughout Poland and to dozens of other countries. Just before the Holocaust began, the movement numbered 70,000 members. After World War II, the movement was revived in Poland and even established a political party that took part in the elections for the Polish Parliament. It was linked to the Craiova Guardia. The movement was dismantled by government orders on March 31, 1949.

TOWER AND STOCKADE – A settlement method used by Zionist settlers in Mandatory Palestine during the 1936-1939 Arab revolt, which established fortified agricultural settlements and kibbutzim that provided safe havens for the Jewish settlers.

YEVSEKTSIYA – Was the Jewish section of the Soviet Communist Party. Established in 1918, its mission was to destroy traditional Jewish life, the Zionist movement and its youth organizations and Hebrew culture, and to replace them with "proletarian culture." Following World War II, the Polish Communist Party adopted the name and organization to oppose the Zionist movements in Poland, until their total elimination in 1950.

THE ESCAPE MOVEMENT – Was a Zionist initiative that operated between 1944-1948 and was responsible for the illegal immigration of nearly 300,000 Holocaust survivors to Eretz Yisrael, after World War II ended.

ZVI NETZER – One of the leading figures in Poland of the post-war illegal immigration operation to Eretz Yisrael, the *Mosssad L'Aliyah Bet*, and head of the Escape Movement in Poland between 1946-1948. He was later an active leader in *Nativ*, an organization that encouraged Jews behind the Iron Curtain to make *aliyah* to Israel.

HENRYK JABŁOŃSKI – Professor of History at Warsaw University, member of the Academy of Sciences, later became a politician and served as President of Poland from 1972-1985.

UNION OF POLISH PATRIOTS – Established by Wanda Wasilewska, a Polish left-wing political activist who was close to Stalin. This union was parallel to the right-wing temporary Polish government in London. The first Polish Army, created within the Russian army's framework towards the end of the war, was known as the Wanda Army.

GENERAL ZYGMUND BERLING – Commander of the Wanda Army, which fought on the Eastern Front of World War II.

GENERAL WŁADYSŁAW ANDERS – A Polish general, commander of the Polish Division that was organized in Russia and left for Palestine with a hundred thousand Poles and Jews, journeying through Teheran to Palestine and the Arabian desert to fight alongside the British army.

KWAMPINSKI – The political representative in Tashkent of the Polish government-in-exile in London.

MORDECHAI ROSMAN AND MOTAK ROTMAN – Leaders of Hashomer Hatzair in Asia. They were nicknamed the 'Asians.' After World War II ended, they – together with Abba Kovner – were partisans in the forests of Vilna and established the Escape Movement from Poland.

COLONEL RODNITSKI – One of the high commanders of the Anders Army, who was in contact with the Jewish Agency in Teheran.

MARSHAL KONSTANTIN ROKOSSOVSKY – Commander of the 2nd Belarus front and led Operation Bagration that emancipated Belarus from the Nazis. Took part in the Battle of Berlin.

MARSHAL GEORGY ZHUKOV – Commander of the 1st Belarus front and the Battle of Berlin, which resulted in the defeat of Nazi Germany and the end of World War II.

JAKUB (YAACOV) BERMAN – Member of the Polish Politburo. Was in charge of Poland's military, internal and external security agencies after World War II.

JÓZEF CYRANKIEWICZ – Prime Minister of Poland after World War II (1947-1952).

Made in United States
Troutdale, OR
04/16/2024